PERCEIVING THE INVISIBLE

MELINDA H. CONNOR

D.D. Ph.D. AMP FAM

OTHER BOOKS BY MELINDA H. CONNOR

TEN DAILY NEEDS

ACCESSING HIGHER TRUTH

RESONANCE MODULATION: BIOFIELD BASICS

ADVANCED BODY READING

CASETAKING FOR THE ENERGY PRACTITIONER

PROFESSIONAL PRACTICE FOR THE ENERGY HEALING PRACTITIONER

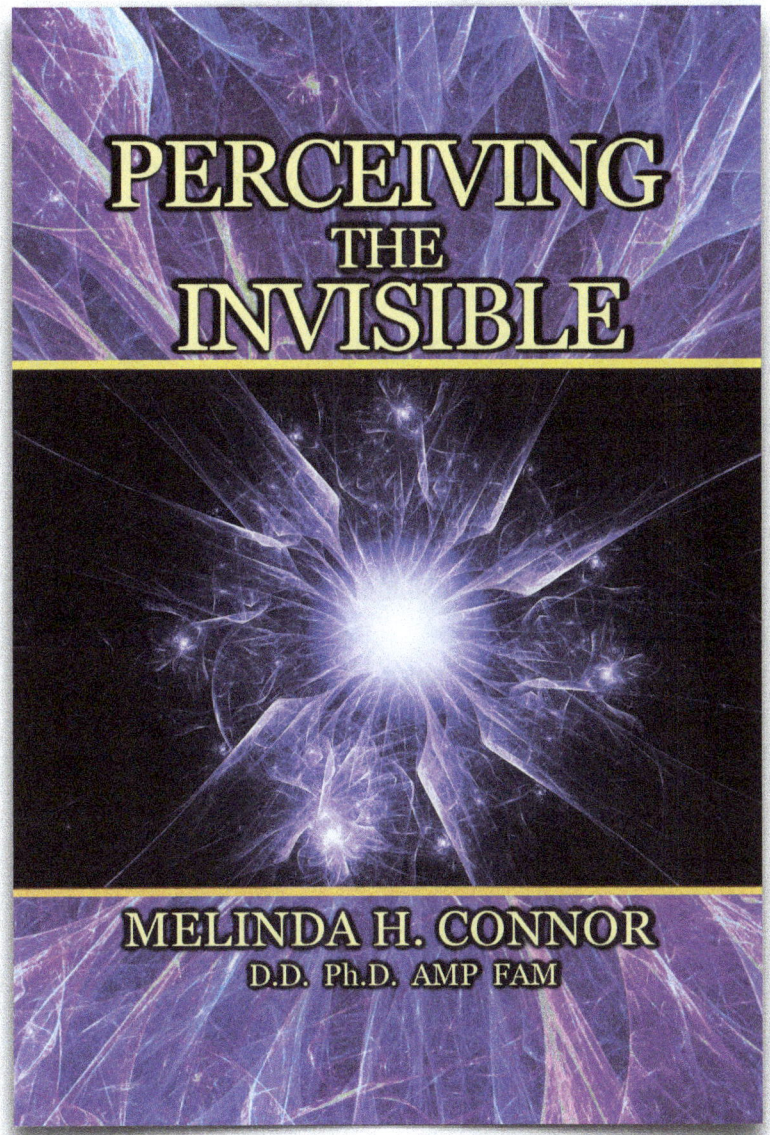

The material contained in this book has been written for informational purposes and is not intended as a substitute for medical advice, nor is it intended to diagnose, treat, cure, or prevent disease. If you have a medical issue or illness, consult a qualified physician.

Published by

ARNICA PRESS
www.ArnicaPress.com

Copyright © 2009, 2025 Melinda H. Connor

Written by Melinda H. Connor
Photos by Melinda H. Connor

Cover Photo: Shutterstock

Manufactured in the United States of America

ISBN: 978-1-955354-80-6

All rights reserved. No part of this book may be reproduced or transmitted in any form or by any means, electronic or mechanical, including photocopying, recording, or by any information storage and retrieval system, without the prior written permission from the Author. This book may not be AI scraped or utilized in AI processes unless permission in writing is received by the author.

THE DISCLAIMER
PLEASE READ BEFORE READING THE BOOK

The information presented in this book is educational in nature and is provided only as general information. As part of the information contained in this book, you understand you will be introduced to processes and exercises for the purpose of learning how to experience the auric field intuitively, kinesthetically, and visually. The author and publisher do not know how you will personally respond to learning about auras and using the information about auras contained in this book. You agree to assume and accept full responsibility for any and all risks associated with reading this book and using the information contained in this book.

The author and publisher accept no responsibility or liability whatsoever for the use or misuse of the information contained in this book. By continuing to read this book, you knowingly, voluntarily, and intelligently assume these risks, including any adverse outcome that might result from experiencing the auric field and/or using the information contained in this book about auras, and agree to release, indemnify, hold harmless and defend the author and publisher, and their respective heirs, agents, consultants, and employees from and against any and all claims which you, or your heirs and/or representatives, may have for any loss, damage, or injury of any kind or nature arising out of or in connection with reading this book. If any court of law rules that any part of this Disclaimer is invalid, the Disclaimer stands as if those parts were struck out

**BY CONTINUING TO READ THE BOOK
YOU AGREE TO THE DISCLAIMER**

PLEASE ENJOY THE BOOK AND HAVE FUN!

To Sean Regean
I love you, my friend. I too wish the world were different.

And to Lisa Leonard,
who was at the birth of this book and I hope is watching over it now.
Know that we love you and saw the many things of value which you did
for people,
the beautiful gifts which you brought to the world
and the many changes which you made in you. Journey safely.

ACKNOWLEDGMENTS

I am so excited for the new version of this book to be birthed. The original version took 10 years from putting words on a page to production. This version has taken several months as over the years of writing additional books I finally developed my own method. For this edition I would like to thank Sabrina Mesko founder of Arnica Publishing for her wisdom, kindness and amazing new cover. As always Kendra Gains for all things editing of drafts, I am so glad you are my friend. To Betsy Lehrfeld for all things legal, you are a blessing in my life. Gary, I kept your forward in this edition as I love the pieces of the science on the biofield that you shared. To all the folks who aided in the original book much gratitude. I hope that this version of the book will bring those who read it much joy and development of the correct skills. You saw the field as a child. Give yourself the gift of seeing the field again. It is a God given right.

FOREWORD
BY Gary E. Schwartz, Ph.D.

If I hadn't believed it, I wouldn't have seen it.
Yogi Berra

There was a time that I believed that seeing auras was like seeing striped elephants. If someone told you she was seeing a striped elephant floating above your head, you might wonder whether she was joking, on drugs, or mentally ill. If a child reported seeing an aura, I was taught to interpret it as a sign of youthful imagination, poor eyesight, or psychopathology. Case closed.

However, advances in contemporary scientific theory and research, coupled with my own personal experiences – including working with Dr. Melinda Connor, the inspired author of this book – I have come to the conclusion that there is more to seeing auras than merely belief or imagination.

Yes, being open to the possibility that auras are real increases the probability that you will be able to experience them. And yes, having a creative imagination appears to facilitate being able to see them. However, the capacity to see the richness and complexity of auras, the ability to interpret their significance, and the skills involved in using this information in diagnosis and treatment, involve more than openness and creativity. It requires knowledge and training. *Perceiving the Invisible* provides an introduction to this remarkable human capacity.

In my book *The Energy Healing Experiments*, I describe laboratory studies that demonstrate:

1. Untrained people can detect energy fields/biofields, even if they are unaware that they have this capacity.

2. Health professionals can be trained to detect energy fields. Moreover, the personality dimension of openness and absorption predicts individual differences in people's facility in learning energy detection.

3. All living things generate coherent patterns of light that are typically invisible to the naked eye (i.e. auras). It is possible to record these patterns of light using a low light CCD camera cooled to -100 degrees centigrade. Using this camera, we have demonstrated that plants, for example, generate subtle patterns of light that extend beyond their physical boundaries and interconnect their neighbors with a complex web or matrix of light.

4. People who claim to be able to see auras and make medical diagnoses from a distance (called medical intuitives) can obtain accurate information about a patient's medical condition in a double blind experiment.

This laboratory research is consistent with Dr. Connor's thesis concerning the reality and value of seeing auras. However, what was especially significant for me was participating in an introductory workshop taught by Dr. Connor where I learned how to see auras myself. Mindful of the possibility that I might be engaged in creative fantasy, I put my emerging visions to the test and discovered that I could use this information for diagnostic purposes. There is no substitute for direct personal experience.

Dr. Connor is not only a gifted seer and healer; she is a well trained scientist specializing in complimentary and alternative medicine. Looking at it from a neuropsychological viewpoint, not only does she appear to manifest highly developed left and right hemispheric processing, she shows evidence of highly developed corpus callosum (integrative) processing as well.

Perceiving the Invisible is not only informative and authoritative, it is fun. May you enjoy the process of discovering auras with Dr. Connor as much as I have done.

Gary E. Schwartz, Ph.D.

Professor of Psychology, Medicine, Neurology, Psychiatry and Surgery, and Director of the Laboratory for Advances in Consciousness and Health, at the University of Arizona. Also Corporate Director of Development of Energy Healing at Canyon Ranch Resorts. Author of The Energy Healing Experiments.

Table of Contents

Disclaimer 5
Acknowledgments 9
Foreword by Gary E. Schwartz, Ph.D. 11
Introduction 19

CHAPTER ONE ~ The Breath 27
The Breath 27
Practice a square breath 32
Space to practice 35

CHAPTER TWO ~ Grounding 37
Grounding 37
Grounding meditation 40
Quick recap - grounding 47

CHAPTER THREE ~ Intention Setting 49
Intention setting 49
Intention meditation 50
Why set an intention? 53
Why be precise when I set an intention? 53
Quick recap - setting an intention 54
Review questions 55

CHAPTER FOUR ~ Midline Current 57
Midline current 57
What is the goal of this practice?......................................58
Learning to feel the Midline meditation 58
Already feeling the Midline meditation 59
Quick recap - feeling the Midline....................................60
Single point of focus body experience.............................61
The next level..62
Quick recap - single point of focus..................................63
Intention setting at the Midline current..........................64
Perceiving the current flow - Intention setting..............64
Clearing the current flow - Intention setting 65
The process to this point 66

CHAPTER FIVE ~ The Chakra System 67
The Chakra system 67
Placement of the "big" nerve plexus/chakras.................72
Meditation to open flow in 6th chakra............................76
Meditation to clear the tips of the 6th and 7th chakras........77
Meditation to increase spin in 6th chakra......................77
Meditation to increase the flow in 7th chakra 80
Combine 6th and 7th chakras..80
Meditation on the covers Chakra system.......................81
Quick recap - Chakra flow 83

CHAPTER SIX ~ Clearing the Noise 85
Clearing the noise...88
Meditation to clear the veils..88

CHAPTER SEVEN ~ Arcs of Light 89
Arcs of Light..89
Meditation to Stimulate the Pineal and Pituitary..........90

Recap – Arcs of Light 93

CHAPTER EIGHT ~ Looking through the forehead
Looking through the forehead 95
Meditation of "switching up" 95
Quick recap - switching up 99

CHAPTER NINE ~ Stages of seeing 101
Stages of seeing 101
Review - stages of seeing 110

CHAPTER TEN ~ Obstacles to seeing 111
Obstacles to seeing 111
The fear of seeing the auric field 111
The potential abuse of power 113
They think I am different? 114
But I just had to tell them 115
No, I don't want to 116
Longing 117
Rage 118

CHAPTER ELEVEN ~ Ethics of seeing 121
Ethics of seeing 121
Quick recap - Ethical check list 129

CHAPTER TWELVE ~ Other methods of perceiving the Auric field 131
Other methods of perceiving the Auric field 131
Quick recap 139
Final review 140
About the Author 143

INTRODUCTION

Welcome to seeing auras! There is no mystery to seeing the auric field if you understand the process involved. Everyone is capable of seeing the field if you are willing to practice. From the observations that I have made and the study of the brain that I have done, I now believe that the ability to see the field structures which surround and penetrate through the body is actually an older visual system of the body. It is not primarily shorter/high frequency waves that you see, instead it is longer waves that you see with more complete vision. One of the benefits of seeing the field is that you can "see in the dark." All you have to do to see in the additional frequency ranges involved, is put the body's current in the correct spot in the brain and that happens by using your breath and focus as tools. Sounds simple doesn't it! Well, it is. Practice and you will be well on your way to reclaiming skills that have been lost in our modern age.

Thousands of years in the past, as we evolved, we needed skills that allowed us to compete for food, help keep us safe and make choices that allowed us to survive and thrive. Loosing skills that other species have, was not a good survival choice. Think of seeing the field as a good survival choice for hunters. Those people who could perceive the animal they were seeking for food, survived longer. Those people who could perceive danger and protect themselves, could survive longer. Seeing the field of beings around you allows you to do both. In the modern world we do not need skills in those areas in the same way. So, we are losing or dismissing what was necessary for survival as it is not as important. I prefer to have all the tools I might need. The world is changing. From climate changes, to globalization, to privation, a range of skills in any population is necessary for survival.

There are lots of ways to "see' the field. You can see it through taste, smell, touch, cognitive sensing, intuitive sensing, the list goes on. There are as many ways to sense as there are people on earth, as each person is a work of art unto themselves. However, this book is specific to the visual sensing process of "seeing the field."

I would like to note that this book has been written primarily for the energy healing practitioner who is in professional practice. It is for the practitioner who needs a specific, accurate and professional book with which to do additional skills building. It is not been written for a popular audience. There are a number of books available to the public on this topic. (Most of those are wildly incorrect calling after images from fixating the eyes "seeing the auric field.") Real "seeing the field" is seeing outside of the frequencies of normal physical vision through your eyes. And you can mix those frequencies with those of the eyes but it these older frequencies are "seen" through a different process.

If you are a healer in professional practice, you can already perceive the field. Since that is the case, why bother with learning to see? It is just more information. Exactly! That is precisely the reason to do the skills building. It is more information. It is a great deal of information and it is very accurate. Your client may say one thing but their field will show you the truth. The truth will help in the client's journey toward health. This book is primarily targeted at the kinesthetic professional practitioner, though it can be used by anyone with trained extended sensing skills so that they have another tool to help their clients.

I have discovered that almost all children under the age of two can see the auric field. I travel a great deal and one of the things that I love to do in airports when I am waiting for a plane is take some light out of my heart, put it in a ball and toss it up in the air. All of the very small children in the gate area will laugh and clap when they see it fly around. Parents are happy because their children are not fussy for a few minutes and I have lots of fun entertaining them. I love to watch as their faces light up. I love to watch the freedom with which they respond to a natural and normal process.

My current theory is that everyone begins life with the ability to see the auric field, but we lose this capacity as we grow older. In our society we do not need the skill of seeing the field to survive and it is not a "normal" behavior in most families today. We are almost taught not to see. However, following these lessons, and with practice, you will reawaken this lost natural ability. In this manual we will focus on the process of seeing the auric field, or as I prefer to call it, the Biofield. We will not be seeing through your physical eyes, though you can add that visual system to your mix. Instead, we will be "switching up" to using the brain area to "see." We will be seeing through a set of nerve plexuses that are in the brain. We will not be focusing on seeing the fields intuitively or kinesthetically, though these are good ways of perceiving as well. And again, that information can be mixed in.

The process of seeing the field begins with the breath. The breath is the fire; the breath creates the flow. Without breath your body cannot survive. Your body is an electrical-chemical-magnetic environment. The breath that you take into your body triggers and generates the chemical reaction between the waters of the body and the oxygen you are drawing into your body. The hydrogen-oxygen burn combine with body chemistry and the three-dimensional magnetic field produced by the body to create the powering of the body.

Here is some background, our bodies are a three-dimensional physical electro-magnetic environment. Nerves produce electrical current. Any electrical system that exists for any length of time, produces a magnetic field. Our cells are closer to sea water than to pure water. Sea water which is placed in three-dimensional fields will burn. That is hard science work done by Dr. Rustum Roy and John Kanzious. So, part of the power system of the body is this burn. Regardless of how the process actually happens, it does happen. It is through the "burn" that the current that is necessary to see the auric/biofield field is generated. To see the field, you have to get enough power, enough electrical stimulation, to the correct spots in the brain to trigger a hormonal release which in turn stimulates the correct sets of nerves and opens your visual system to another set of frequencies.

So, to power the process we will begin with breathing.
Melinda

Trees have fields too!

BY THE END OF THE BOOK YOU SHOULD BE ABLE TO DO THIS WHOLE PROCESS!

1. BREATHE AND CHARGE THE BODY.
2. GROUND AND CHARGE THE BODY MORE.
3. SET AN INTENTION IF YOU CHOOSE.
4. LET THE CURRENT FLOW UP THE MIDLINE CURRENT OF THE BODY.
   OR
   RUN ARCHES OF LIGHT FROM THE BASE OF THE PELVIC FLOOR TO THE FRONT OF THE HEAD AND THE BACK OF THE HEAD.

5. LET THE CURRENT MEET AT THE PENAL AND THE PITUITARY GLANDS IN THE BRAIN.
6. ALLOW THAT AREA TO CHARGE UNTIL THERE IS A HORMONAL RELEASE.
7. LET THAT HORMONAL RELEASE STIMULATE THE NERVE PLEXUS IN THE FRONTAL LOBE AND THE OCCIPITALUS REGION OF THE BRAIN.
8. SWITCH UP THE TO LOOKING THROUGH THOSE NERVE PLEXUS.
9. SEE WHAT YOU SEE!

CHAPTER ONE

THE BREATH

Most people do not breathe adequately; they are shallow breathers. Because there is insufficient breath there isn't enough fuel for the process of seeing. The long deep slow breath that causes the upper chest to rise and the lower rib cage to widen is the type of breath we want to achieve.

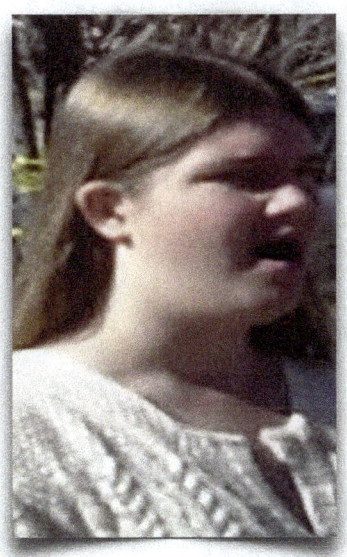

A "Singer's Breath" is one of the best ways to breathe.
It is good for the body and brain!

The breath is the fire, the breath is the flow, and the breath helps to generate the currents of the body. It is important to consider that how you breathe makes the difference in the amount of oxygen you take into the body. If your upper chest is tight, you get a smaller breath. If your belly is too tight you take in less breath because the diaphragm cannot move freely. If your shoulders are locked you take in less breath. Relaxing and becoming aware of where your body is tight is the first step in allowing the body to take in more air.

Start by taking in a breath. Can you feel any space where your body is tight? Many people as a result of having very busy lives tighten their neck and shoulder area. Check that area first. Feel in to your neck and your shoulders. Do they feel tight? Take a moment and touch your neck and your shoulders. Do they feel tight under your fingers? If they do you might consider rolling your shoulders or gently massaging your shoulders and neck. Roll your head from side to side in a very gentle movement. Do not move so sharply that you generate pain.

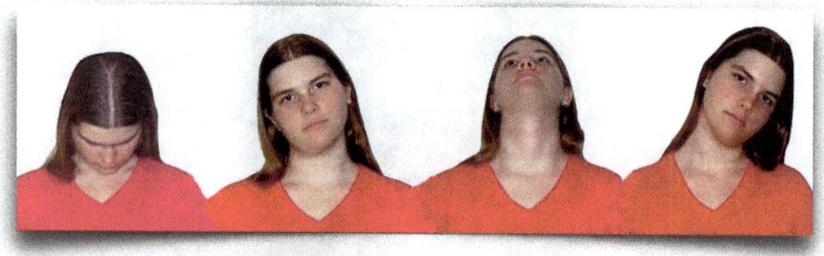

Swing your shoulders forward and then let them fall naturally.

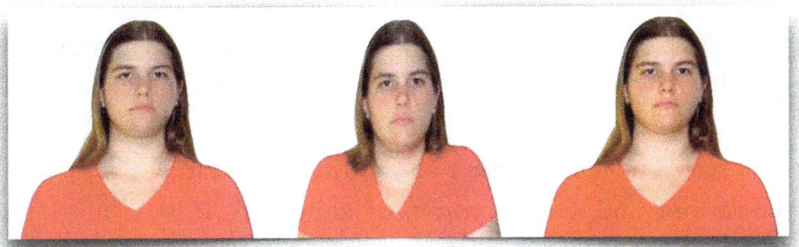

If you are able stretch your arms above your head,
do so and then stretch them out to your sides.

Can you feel your neck and shoulders begin to loosen? You can repeat these movements but do them gently. Once you have checked your neck and shoulders feel into your tummy.

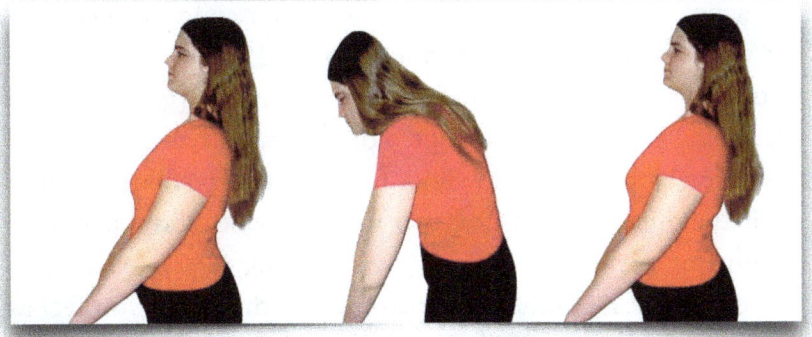

Stretch gently back and then bend forward rounding your body. Then stretch gently back again and then straighten.

Do not push your body to the point of pain. Just stretch it gently. This will help to loosen the chest and tummy muscles. Once you have stretched, then practice taking a breath. Can you feel your tummy move as you breathe? Can you feel your chest rise and fall as you take a breath? If you need to practice further, try looking in a mirror and watching as you take a breath. See how your chest moves. See how your tummy moves. Enjoy the process of your body stretching into a fresher form of taking a breath.

As you practice breathing, allow yourself to use your imagination as a tool. Imagine that when you're breathing in, you are breathing in all the way to the belly. Imagine that when you breathe in, you fill out both your front into the tummy and back into the back. Imagine that the breath comes through the nose, or through the mouth, or both, down through the windpipe, filling the lungs, and then filling the body. There is a brief pause that takes place, once that breath has filled the space, and then the exhale is gentle and smooth with the air clearing back out of that space.

Practice breathing slowly. Begin on a four count; you can use a watch or metronome if you choose. Practice breathing in for a count of four, pausing for a count of one, and then exhaling for a count of four. If you can inhale, pause, and exhale slightly more slowly -- for example, a count of eight for the inhale, a count of two for the pause, and a count of eight for the exhale -- that's a good thing to try. Gradually over time, it is useful to deepen the breath so that you feel as if the belly is filling fully. Physiologically, of course, the lungs are filling and the diaphragm is being moved in its position, which shifts the feeling in the belly. But perceptually, and for the purposes of the focus, allow your imagination to become a tool and imagine that the breath is actually flowing into the belly. Once you reach the point where you can breathe in for a count of four, pause for one, and exhale for a count of four, you can begin to practice grounding. But do endeavor to reach the point where you can breathe in for four, pause for one, and exhale for four.

Over time, shift your breathing to long slow breaths so you move from a four count to an eight, then to a twelve count. A singer or someone trained in how to breathe can go all the way up to twenty! Controlling the breath helps to increase the amount of current flow in the body. Such deep long slow inhales and exhales are not requirements to seeing the field; however, this will increase the amount of raw material available to create the current flow. More current flow supports the body's ability to see accurately and fully. Set your goal of improving your deep slow breathing and, gently over time, your lung capacity will develop as will your improved sight.

Practice a Square Breath

1. Breathe in for a count of four.
2. Count as slowly as you are comfortable doing while you breathe. Keep you counts evenly spaced.
3. Hold your breath for a count of four.
4. Exhale for a count of four.
5. Hold the exhale for a count of four.
6. Repeat

Remember, slowly build up to the four counts inhale, exhale and the holds. Be gentle with yourself and do not do more than your body is ready to do.

Some of you may have challenges to overcome, such as asthma, allergies, or bronchitis; you might consider working with a professional to help develop your breathing. A respiratory therapist is specifically trained in developing the breath and would be an excellent choice. Those of you without medical conditions but still needing help might seek a vocal coach; although trained with a different focus and purpose, the end result will be the same. Singers are specifically trained in proper breathing and it could be fun to learn to breathe with a singing coach. Who knows, you may find you have a new career in singing.

CAUTION!

IT IS EASY TO HYPERVENTILATE WHEN DOING BREATHING EXERCISES. IT IS WISE TO DO YOUR BREATHING SLOWLY AND GENTLY.

IF YOU FEEL THAT YOU ARE GETTING DIZZY, STOP AND WAIT SEVERAL MINUTES UNTIL YOUR BREATHING RETURNS TO A MORE NORMAL PATTERN AND THE DIZZINESS CLEARS.

IT IS NOT USEFUL TO YOU TO PRACTICE BREATHING TO THE POINT THAT YOU BECOME DIZZY; YOU WON'T BE ABLE TO SEE THE AURIC FIELD.

Below is a picture of the Breath Path. The arrows represent the path the breath will follow. Moving in through the nose, it moves down the windpipe and into the lungs. There are little sacs called alveoli that bring the oxygen to the blood. Then the blood circulates through the body and feeds oxygen to the cells. Oxygen is the fuel that allows our cells to function. So oxygen is our critical energy source and your lungs act as a set of bellows. These bellows fan the fire and the flow; then, as the current grows, it aids the process of seeing. So *breathe* consciously, and enjoy it!

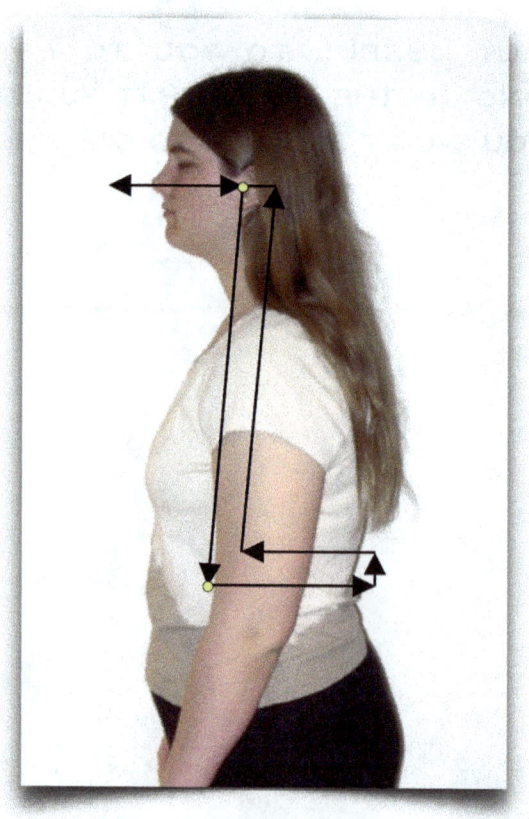

SPACE TO PRACTICE

To begin the process of the practice of seeing the auric field, one first needs to have the correct tools. You need a quiet space so that you can focus and spend sufficient time uninterrupted. I suggest a half-hour of practice two to three times a week. As you begin to see, you can add seeing auras to any part of your day, without necessarily needing the quiet space in which to focus.

Uninterrupted time is another useful practice tool. Develop a dedicated time each day, giving yourself a specific schedule to which you can commit. In order to develop sufficient current flow it is useful to practice seeing the auric/biofield field for a period of thirty minutes or more in the early stages of your practice. Find a place to sit where the light is slightly dimmed. Initially, because the power current is not as high when you actually begin to see the auric/biofield field, it will appear in shimmers, and it is easier to see shimmers in a room that has slightly dimmed light.

As color starts to come in you may find it just looks as if the light has changed a little bit. It may appear slightly rosy or to have a yellowish tint or cast, kind of like looking at the room through a piece of colored cellophane. It is useful to have a white sheet, white paper, or white wall to hold your hand in front of, looking at the edges of your hand to see the auric/biofield field.

CHAPTER TWO

GROUNDING

Once you reach the point where you can inhale for a count of four, pause for a count of one, and exhale for a count of four, you are ready to begin the process of grounding. An ability to breathe longer than a count of four, is a plus going into the grounding practice. If, in fact, you can breathe in as long as a count of eight, twelve, sixteen, or twenty, so much the better, because with the deepening of the breathing, you increase the amount of the current flow. As you deepen the breathing into the belly, you also increase the feeling of the current flow throughout the entire body. Flow and an increase of the current are necessary in the process of grounding.

What is grounding? Grounding is the method of drawing energy into the body from a nonhuman source like the earth. Everyone does that to a greater or lesser extent every moment of his or her life. The difference in this situation is that we will make it a conscious practice. You need to know and feel that you are drawing current. An awareness of drawing the current is very important. In addition to adding more current to the body, it is also a way of focusing the mind.

The grounding current of the earth can also be called a piezio electric current. The different parts of the Earth's crust turn at different rates. The surface plates move more slowly than the liquid mantle on which they sit. The iron crystalline core of the earth moves faster than the mantle. The neutrino cloud that houses the consciousness of the earth and sits in the center of the crystalline core moves faster yet. All of the subtle rotations help to keep our earth together and create an alternating electrical current. This frequency measures from 6.8Hz to 7Hz.

When you are working with the energies using the biggest field available, You are charging your body quickly and effortlessly. In addition, doing things easily has the continued benefit of helping your breathing relax and your body to relax.

Let us begin by looking at how you are going to use your mind to create the state of being grounded. The mind is a tool. The mind recognizes patterns and it recognizes the history of a pattern. The mind can focus the energies. We are going to concentrate on using the mind to create a focus point. In focusing the mind, we will look at visualization, imagination, and breath, as tools to aid and power that focus.

One of my friends is fond of saying, "It isn't real unless you feel," and that should be the watchword here. At any step of the exercises, if you're not feeling the process in your body, do not continue to the next step until you can. Work with it. Many times, one can be working with a particular exercise and it takes two to three times of doing the exercise before you will feel solid body awareness develop. Allow yourself that time, and trust the fact that you have the capacity to feel these processes in your body. Until you can feel the process in your body you will have difficulty in manipulating the process to charge the body correctly. So practice and enjoy the awakening of body sensation.

In my experience, every child has the ability and is actively seeing the auric/biofield field. When I play with children who are year and two years old, I often take my auric fingers and tickle their tummy. Without exception, they all giggle, and start to grab for the auric fingers. So it is my opinion that every child sees. Seeing is a natural process and can be lots of fun!

Grounding is about receiving energy from the earth to nurture the self. One receives energy from the earth to feed the energetic flow of current that moves through the body. In addition, one can receive energy from the sun, the moon, the sky, the plants and all living things around us, from God. It is a normal and regular occurrence. Think of it this way. If you eat a candy bar, you are putting food into your body that then creates nourishment necessary for the body to keep functioning. So just like feeding the body food to give it energy for continued function, grounding also feeds the body energy directly for continued function and, in fact, can increase the amount of energy in the body. Most people who ground find they are full of energy.

To begin the process of grounding by receiving energy into the body from the ground or the divine, or the sun or the trees, the sky, the water, the moon, we must allow ourselves and our bodies to move into a receptive state. This is similar to a radio station installing a more powerful transmitter so that you can hear its signal better. Receiving energy from the Earth into the body transmitted at a bigger rate, a higher level of transmission, like through the radio station's stronger transmitter, gives one a better signal. And that's the purpose, to get the best signal possible. Again, we're going to work with imagination as a tool. Practice this lesson regularly until you can feel the current coming into your body.

GROUNDING MEDITATION

Begin with the breath. Allow the breath to flow into the body. Breathe slowly and fully, at least on a four count, and if you can go longer, do so. Take three very deep breaths and exhale them in sequence. Breathe in for four, pause for one to four, and exhale for four. Breathe in for four, pause for one to four, and exhale for four. Breathe in for four, pause for one, and exhale for four. Let the worries and troubles of the day dissolve away.

Put your feet flat on the floor. If you are standing, bounce gently on your feet. Really allow yourself to feel your feet on the floor. If you are in a place where you can do it comfortably, do this without shoes so you can feel the pressure of the floor against your feet. If you are sitting in a chair, make sure that your feet can touch the floor. If you are sitting on the floor, fold your knees up so that the bottoms of your feet can rest directly against the floor.

Feel your feet against the floor and allow your imagination, as a tool, to feel what it would be like if your feet were touching the ground beneath the floor. Imagine that your feet have gotten heavy. Imagine that your feet have fallen right through the floor to the ground below. Now check and see what you feel. Is the ground below you warm or cold? Is the ground wet or dry? Remember use your imagination as a tool. Does the ground feel dusty or rocky, hard or soft? Is it springy or is it wet? How does the ground feel? Wiggle your toes. How does it feel as the toes move through the ground?

Can you feel the dirt/clay/sand/rock move past your toes? Take a moment and let your feet play. What kinds of sensate experiences are you having?

Now take another breath. Breathe in for four, pause for one to four, and out for four. Imagine now that your feet are falling. Your feet are falling until they are ten miles down into the earth. How does that feel? Is it different from the surface? Does it feel warm or cold? Is it still or moving? Does it feel thick or thin, grainy or hard? Take a moment and see how it feels. Try moving your feet around again. Can you feel the rock, water, dirt brushing past your ankles?

Now take another breath. Breathe in for four, pause for one to four, and exhale for four. Using your imagination, allow yourself to envision an iron ball at the center of the Earth. Let your feet drop. Just watch as they fall. There is nothing to do. Just watch them fall. Then slide your feet over the iron crystalline core. How do your feet feel? Is the core rough or is it smooth? Does it snag at your feet or do you feel as if your feet are sliding on a glassy surface. Then slide your feet inside that iron ball.

Is the ball warm or cold? Is it thick or thin? How solid is it? What is in the center? Does it feel open or tight? Does it feel charged or still?

Allow yourself to watch what your body does when you say to yourself, I'm grounding into the etheric, I'm grounding into the auric, I'm grounding into the astral. Just watch and see how you feel different.

Grounding to the etheric is grounding into the etheric bodies, the subtle bodies of the human body. The etheric bodies are the echoes, the

harmonics, of the weak Van der Wals forces that stick the water molecules of your body together. They look kind of like a grid pattern. It is not exactly square but it is generally even unless there is a pull or tears in the charged field.

Similar to the grid pattern of the structured layers.

Grounding into the auric is grounding into the auric/biofield field. What is the auric/biofield made of? Well, your body inhales oxygen and exhales all sorts of gasses through your skin. Your skin is the biggest organ of your body. Each of your organs has both an electric and magnetic field that it produces. Did you know that your heart produces the largest magnetic field in the body? These electrical and magnetic fields extend past the surface of the body for several inches. With special instruments like a Super Quantum Interference Detector (SQUID), you can measure and map these fields. Then each of your nerves produces an electrical field. At every place where you have a set of nerve endings coming together, they form what is called a nerve plexus. Because nerves do not fire evenly and in sequence, the electrical field that they produce turns or is "torsioned." These are just some of the things that make of the Biofield. It is the field made up by the biological process of the body and it extends past the surface of the body.

Grounding into the astral is grounding into the layers of the heart. As mentioned, the heart produces the largest magnetic field of the body. The body is very sensitive to magnetic current. When you connect to the magnetic field of the heart you help that magnetic charge to be distributed all over the body to keep the body healthy.

Now take another breath. Breathe in for four, pause for one to four, and breathe out for four. Again, use your imagination as a tool. Allow yourself to imagine that the energy from the iron core of the earth is coming back up into your feet. Let yourself relax into receiving. Just watch the current come into your body. Energy moves like water from the highest gradient or concentration to the lowest gradient or concentration. Another way of saying it is that energy rolls down hill. Since you are human you do not have as big a field as the Earth. That means that you are a lower concentration than the Earth. So the Earth's energy will just roll down hill into you if you will let it. See if you can feel the current as it comes into your feet. Try to feel it as the flow of the energy as it comes into the ankles and begins to rise up through the legs, through the calves, into the knees, through the knees into the thighs, and into the hips. Allow yourself to breathe, and allow the energy just to flow.

Check in with how the flow is coming in your feet. Is the current as wide as the bottom of your foot? If it is not as wide as the bottom of your foot, allow the current to get wider. Just watch as it opens and relaxes.

Does it feel good? Allow yourself to sink into the experience of the full current coming into your feet just as it did when you were a small child.

This is also an opportunity to practice focusing your mind. Become an observer, just like you would as a scientist or investigator. Watch what happens when the energy flows. How does it feel as it flows up the torso and into the belly? How does it feel as it fills up the chest and sinks into each cell, replenishing and restoring the body? Allow the energy to continue to flow, and as you're watching the energy flow up the body, you might also look to see how wide the flow is coming into your legs. Is it narrower than your calf, or is it as wide as your thigh?

Again, using your imagination as a tool, envision that the flow is as wide as the thigh as it moves up the body. Just like a flow of water fills to the banks as a stream widens, allow the current to flow and fill the body. And watch how much faster your body receives the energy up the body.

Now allow the energy to flow through the body, through the torso up the neck and through the head, and fountain out of the head and back down over the body, just as if you were standing in the middle of a water fountain on a nice, warm, sunny day. Let the energy wash over the body and through the body. Imagine that each cell is being washed by the energy coming down from your head and flowing back in to the earth. And breathe.

Receiving energy in this way is called *grounding*. You are receiving the energy from the ground, from the earth. When I speak of grounding throughout the book, this is the specific process that I am referring to, receiving energy from the ground through the body and letting it spill back all over the body.

Many people who practice grounding do so by going up into the higher realms. While this is one way of grounding, it does not give you access to the largest frequency set or range available to the human body. I encourage people as they begin this practice of grounding to go down into the Earth so that later they can go up to the skies with lots more power available to them. You can modify this grounding practice to move into any specific frequency set. Do consider starting with what will give you the most range and flexibility.

Many people who practice grounding use the image of receiving current into the tail bone. This is a lovely way of receiving current into the body but it has a drawback. The tail bone is about a half inch in diameter or smaller for most people. The feet are much bigger. Using the feet allows the body to charge faster and more fully. The feet are also pitched lower in frequency set than the tip of the tail bone. This translates to being able to access a broader range of frequencies. It means that you will be able to see more fully, more accurately and more completely.

Practice grounding several times a day. In a week to two weeks with practice, you will even be able to walk and stay grounded. With more practice you can walk up stairs and even run while you stay grounded. Most people experience greater energy and a developing feeling of freedom as their body stays grounded.

QUICK RECAP ~ GROUNDING

1. Feel your feet on the floor.
2. Let your feet fall through the floor into the earth below.
3. Let your feet fall through the earth all the way to the center of the iron core of the earth.
4. Relax and observe as you say to yourself: I am grounding into the etheric. I am grounding into the auric. I am grounding into the astral.
5. Allow the current that starts to flow back up your energy feet and legs to come into your physical body.
6. Let the current get as wide as your feet are wide.
7. Let the current flow freely into your body and let every cell fill up on the current.
8. Let your body fill all the way up through the top of your head and let the excess spill back out through your head and flow over the surface of the body and back into the earth. This allows the Earth to share in your life experience. It's a thank you gift from you to the earth for the beautiful energy that you are receiving.
9. Enjoy the process and let your body charge!

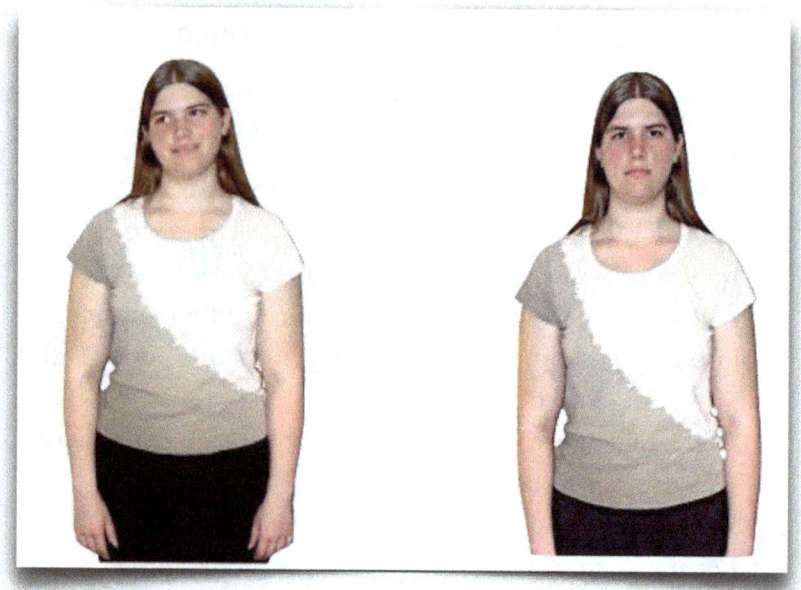

Ungrounded   Grounded

Why are we practicing grounding and staying grounded? We will use this increased flow of current through the body to help the body to charge correctly so that you can see. So practice and enjoy!

CHAPTER THREE

INTENTION SETTING

You can use intention setting to help you see the field in the first place, and then to help you see the field accurately. This is important when you need to look at something you really do not want to see. Most people equate intention setting to using their will to bring something into being. Determination is not the same as manifestation. Neither is wishing, hoping, praying or trusting the same as manifestation. Real intention setting is the "intent to bring that which you wish to manifest into being." It is the first step in the process of manifestation. There is a great deal of popular literature available today on how to set an intention and much of it is flawed.

In the interest of accuracy, I am going to share what my grandmother taught me when I was small. She came from a lineage of women who lived on large estates in Europe and were expected to take care of the people on the estate. She used to make me practice what she called "the weavings" in her rose garden on summer afternoons. She always said that "with correct intention setting and the work of the divine, people can always get well."

The same idea goes for seeing the field. You can also use wishing, hoping, determination and practice. They all help to get the job moving. They are not, however, the same as correct intention setting.

Intention Meditation

Correct intention setting requires a dimensional shift to complete but it begins with the breath. Take a breath and feel into your belly. See if you can feel all the way into the center of the belly just below the tummy button.

If you cannot feel the center of yourself, use imagination as a tool to guide the body's awareness. Breathe into that center of the self just below the tummy button. As you breathe in you may perceive a spark, or an area that feels different, more dense. You may perceive a round circle like a pebble of charged area. Breathe into that central area. Let the breath charge the area more. Relax and keep feeling the area and let each breath flow current into the tummy. Let it flow until the area starts to feel warm inside you or tingly. See the area in your mind's eye. See it filling and spinning. See it starting to sparkle and shine.

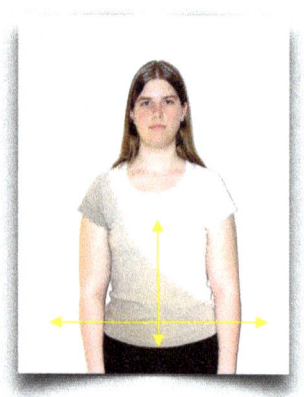

When the area starts to sparkle and shine, use imagination as a tool to guide the body's responses. See a tendril of light flowing up from that sparkle all the way to the heart. Let the light flow freely to the heart and back down into the tummy. Let the heart add its own light. Add beautiful warm heart light twining in to the sparkle from the tummy. As the heart light returns to the tummy let another sparkle, a tendril of light, fall all the way to the earth. Let it fall and thicken so that it is an inch across. Let light from the Earth flow back up this tendril. Let it flow back into the tummy and then flow all the way into the heart. Remember to breath. Relax your shoulders. Relax your back and your tummy.

Allow yourself to enjoy the feeling of the light flowing into the Earth and back into the tummy and the heart. Then let the light upwell and move from the heart all the way through the top of the head. Let it flow up and up and up until you feel it click above your head and begin to move back down into your head, down into your heart, down into your belly, and down into the Earth. Feel the connection above your head to the divine and below you at your feet to the Earth.

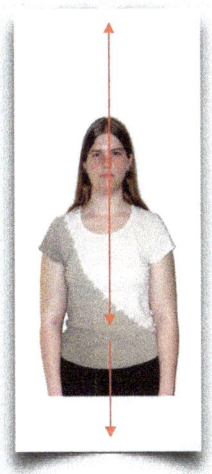

Now sink into contact with the light that is flowing up and down your body. Sink in as if you were lying down in a nice cool river on a summer afternoon. Fall gently into it. Let your consciousness make contact with the flow of current. You may perceive that the light is rosy red in color and warm. From the place of making contact with that current of beautiful rose light, hold that which you will make manifest present. Define it as fully and completely as possible and let it flow into the line of rose light. Watch as it releases, sinks into the rose line of light and then stills for a moment. Watch a moment further and you will see a flash of light like a giant ball flow out from the rose light. It will flash for an instant and then it will settle around you. Your intention has now been set. You may notice as you connected more deeply with this current of rose red light that if you look at anything else in the room it has turned to shades of gray. This is good! It means that you have made contact with the rose red light correctly.

The release is as important as the creation. Allow yourself to release the current of light and feel all of your body more fully again. Become aware of your surroundings and begin to move your body gently. Relax, take a breath and begin to think of other things.

WHY SET AN INTENTION?

It is not required that you set an intention to see the field. Intention setting can help you to see more clearly. It can help you to break more quickly through your fears about what you might see. It can help you to use the information that you see ethically.

WHY BE PRECISE WHEN I SENT AN INTENTION?

The process of creation is additive. Take a look around you. You do not have everything you want manifest in the moment. The universe may be happy to provide but it needs to know what you want. You do not cut away what you do not want. You instead have to list everything you do want and how you want it so that it will get put into the mix. If you are not precise and are careful what you intention for, the universe will manifest it in a very literal fashion and generally not in a way you would expect! Energy takes the path of least resistance.

QUICK RECAP ~ SETTING AN INTENTION

1. Breathe
2. Let the center of the tummy just below the tummy button charge.
3. Let a line of light build from the tummy to the heart.
4. Let the line of light flow back and forth from the tummy to the heart.
5. Let the line of light build and then flow down all the way into the earth.
6. Let the line of light join with Earth light and flow back up through the tummy, through the heart and straight up through the head until you hear it click.
7. Let the light flow up and down from the Earth to the point above the head.
8. Let it get thick and rosy red.
9. Sink into contact with the rosy red line of light.
10. Make manifest your intention as precisely as possible.
11. Watch as the energy build and then releases in a ball around your body.
12. Release contact with the rosy red line of light.
13. Then bring yourself back into contact with your surroundings by moving gently and breathing fully.

Review Questions

Let's take a moment and review just where we are in the process. The first two steps to seeing the field are to breathe and to ground.

Why do we breathe?
Breathing helps to fuel the electrical current of the body. It is necessary to see the field.

Why do we ground?
Because it further charges the field. It gives us a huge raw power source and it helps to control the placement of the electrical flow.

Can we and should we use these techniques for other purposes?
Absolutely! You can use these techniques for anything that you want. It is especially nice to live your life from a place of being grounded. It aids in your clarity and helps to make life fun.

Do I have to use intention setting to see the field?
No. You can use intention setting to support your seeing more accurately but it is not necessary to set an intention to see the field.

How often should I practice breathing and grounding?
At least practice once every day. If possible practice briefly several times a day.

For many people it takes about two weeks of practice to get really grounded. Learning to breathe correctly can take many years. Do not get discouraged. You just need to have some practice at the basics. You do not need to be a pro to see. I have had folks learn to see in a half day class!

CHAPTER FOUR

MIDLINE CURRENT

The next step in learning to see the field is to create a clear path for the current you are generating so that the current can get to the correct place in your body. Once you have reached the point where you can feel the flow of the current through the body, then you are ready to clear the midline current. The midline current is one of the flows of current through the body. It runs more or less straight up and down the center of the body. Just as one flow through the center of a stream can be at a speed and a temperature different from the others, the flow of the midline current through the center of the body, straight from the base of the torso through the top of the head, can also be at a different speed and a different temperature than other current flows of the body.

See if you can feel the center of your body. Can you feel the center line of your body starting from down in the area of the pelvic floor? Start there and looking in a mirror see if you can feel the mid line all the way up through the top of the head. Can you feel it anywhere along that line? Everyone's body is a little different. Some people cannot perceive the midline current at all when they begin the exercise. If you can then you can jump ahead a few paragraphs in the book.

WHAT IS THE GOAL OF THIS PRACTICE?

Current by itself, without getting to the proper place in the body, will not help you see. Being able to develop sufficient body awareness so that you can feel the current flows in the body is the first step in being able to direct the flow of the current. A freely flowing midline current automatically begins to put the correct amount of current into the correct place in the head so that you can begin to see with little effort.

LEARNING TO FEEL THE MIDLINE MEDITATION

If you can't perceive the midline current don't be concerned. Imagine it. Using imagination as your tool, perceive that center current in your body. What would it be like to have a current running straight up your body? How would it feel? How wide would it be? How thick would it be? Where would it start? What would it feel like? Ask yourself these questions.

If you are using imagination as a tool, begin to become aware of your breath again. You need to charge the midline current when you breathe. So let your imagination be the tool to clearing and charging the midline current. Feel the breath flow down through the body on that midline current, clearing the power current as the breath moves. Breathe in through the nose or the mouth, or both if you would like, for a count of four. Imagine the breath flowing right straight down through the power current and clearing out all of the blocks, as if it were a strong warm current going through a dry cold gully, melting all the blocks of ice out of the way, so that the water could move easily and fully through the river valley, through the gully, turning it into an active stream or river.

Remember to breathe, and allow yourself time to learn how to do this. For many people it takes several tries to find the combination of imagination and focusing so that they can allow the mind's focus to move and perceive different sections of the body. You do not have to master this to see the field. However, an awareness of how the current moves through your body will help you to be able to direct the current to the correct place in the body.

ALREADY FEELING THE MIDLINE MEDITATION

If you can feel the current, check on how wide the current is. Is it a half-inch around or an inch wide, is it running straight up your body? Do you feel any curves or bends? If you feel a curve or a bend, can you move the current straight through the bend, either piercing through it, or eroding it away, or just watching the current straighten as it travels through the center of the body? Make contact with that area of the body that has the bend. Breathe into that area. Do you get any images? If so, thank your body and release the images into the light. Does the current run straight now? If not, see if it feel tight or hot, or if it feels stuck. Spend time watching the area and just breathe. Within a minute or two things will move and the area will free up.

Allow yourself to breathe again. See if you can feel any kind of sensation. To begin the process of feeling the sensation of the midline current in the body, again begin with the breath. Breathe in for four, pause for one, and exhale for four. Where to you think your mind is focusing? Is it in your head? Is it in your shoulder? Bring your mind back to the midline current. Check again all the way from the pelvic floor to the top of the head. Can you feel the current actually moving? Where does it move faster? Where does it move slower? If there is any place that does not feel quite free, look at that place more closely. Just watch. Enjoy the experience and breathe.

Quick Recap ~ Feeling the Midline

1. Breathe
2. Feel your seat bones on a chair.
3. Trace the center line of the body in the center of the self from the pelvic floor to the top of the head.
4. Are you aware of it along the full length of the body?
5. Breathe into any place you are not aware of having a sensate reaction.
6. Watch that area until it opens up, unwinds, or clears.
7. Check to see if the current is moving freely.
8. Enjoy the experience of perceiving your body.

SINGLE POINT OF FOCUS BODY EXPERIENCE

Allow yourself to feel your mind. And now, imagine you can move your mind to perceive a different part of your body. For example, how does it feel to experience the tip of your nose from inside yourself? Let your mind focus on feeling the tip of your nose. What is your sensate experience? How does it feel to feel the tip of your tongue?

Take your tongue and put it lightly on the back of your teeth, and feel the tip of your tongue, and breathe again. How does it feel down in your throat? Allow your mind to look at how it feels to feel your throat. How does it feel to swallow? How does it feel to breathe into the chest? How does it feel when the chest moves?

Become an observer and watch how the chest moves, and then switch to feeling it. How does it feel when the chest moves? Move down through the body. Feel and follow the breath flowing down the windpipe and into the lungs. How does it feel when the breath moves into the lungs?

Follow the flow down. Imagine that the breath is flowing into the belly. Now let your mind focus on the belly, and feel the belly itself. How does the belly feel? Does it feel tight? Does it feel loose? Does it feel nervous? Does it feel relaxed? Does it feel warm or cold?

Allow the mind to focus and drop even lower. Follow the breath, the imagined and real current, all the way down to the pelvic floor. Feel down in the pelvic floor. How does it feel?

Is it tight or loose, warm or cold? Is it thick there, is it holding tight, or is it supple? Is it shaky, or is it relaxed?

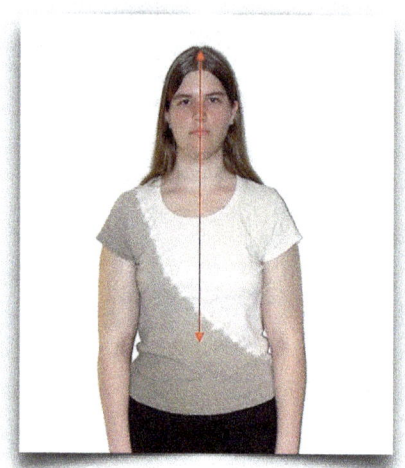

Midline Current

THE NEXT LEVEL

Now, try to feel the midline current again. You've already imagined what it might feel like to feel the power current going through the body. Now that your mind's consciousness is down in the pelvic floor, watch.

Allow yourself to become an observer, and watch as the mind sits and rides on the midline current and slides right back up the body and out through the top of the head. This will help you trace how the midline current in your body is doing. Allow yourself, if you can, to feel your mind moving back up from the pelvis through the body, through the chest, through the neck, through the head and out through the top of the head. When the mind moves that whole length up the body, then begin to practice moving it back down. Move it down the midline current and back up through three or four times. Remember to breathe before, during, and after as you practice moving your mind and your consciousness up and down the body.

As you move your mind up and down the body, watch to see how the breath is doing at melting all the icy boulders from the stream. Allow there to be sufficient breath and sufficient current from the Earth in the body to dissolve the icy boulders from the stream. Just watch as they dissolve, so that there is a smooth flow right straight up the body and out through the top of the head. Even if you can't fully feel the flow from the bottom of the pelvis all the way up through the top of the head, it's all right to continue to the next section. Practice this.

QUICK RECAP – SINGLE POINT OF FOCUS

1. Breathe
2. Pick an area of the body where you wish to focus.
3. Bring your conscious awareness to that area.
4. Breathe into that area of tissue and see how it feels.
5. Check in to see if it is loose or tight. See if it is moving freely.
6. Breathe into the tissue again if it is tight and watch until you can sense movement.
7. Breathe into the tissue while the area moves and opens.
8. Breathe and release and bring your conscious awareness back to everything around you.

INTENTION SETTING AND THE MIDLINE CURRENT

One of the ways that you can speed the process of clearing the midline current of old stored memories and traumas so that the current can move freely, is to use the intention setting techniques we discussed in the last section. Intention setting can also help you to feel the current flow. Intention setting is not a substitute for a free and open current, nor is it a substitute for actually perceiving the current flow. It can, however, help you to achieve both of those things.

PERCEIVING THE CURRENT FLOW - INTENTION SETTING

Begin with the breath. Take three clear, gentle, controlled breaths and let them out fully. Relax your back. Relax your shoulders. Breathe into the center of your tummy just below the tummy button. Let that area begin to charge. As the charge builds let a tendril of light flow into the heart. Then let a tendril of light flow back down to the charged area in the tummy. Let a tendril of light fall to the Earth and let light from the Earth flow back up into the tummy. Let the light move freely between the heart, the tummy and the ground. Then let the light move up through the heart, through the head until it clicks into place above the head. Let the light move freely from the ground all the way to above the head. Sink into contact with the light. Once you have sunk your senses into contact with the lovely rosy red light, still your mind, and see yourself able to perceive any part of your body clearly.

See yourself able to feel each cell in the body. See yourself able to feel the electrical flows of the body whenever you wish. Now breathe and release and allow your awareness to return to the moment.

This is similar to the way a block or stuck place can appear as you are looking at the field.

CLEARING THE CURRENT FLOW - INTENTION SETTING

Begin with the breath. Take three clear, gentle, controlled breaths and let them out fully. Relax your back. Relax your shoulders. Breathe into the center of your tummy just below the tummy button. Let that area begin to charge. As the charge builds let a tendril of light flow into the heart. Then let a tendril of light flow back down to the charged area in the tummy. Let a tendril of light fall to the Earth and let light from the Earth flow back up into the tummy. Let the light move freely between the heart, the tummy and the ground. Then let the light move up through the heart, through the head until it clicks into place above the head. Let the light move freely from the ground all the way to above the head. Sink into contact with the light. Once you have sunk your senses into contact with the lovely rosy red light, still your mind, and see yourself having a clear free flowing current moving up and down the body. See it full and wide, flowing and feeding the body in a way that the body feels joyously. Now breathe and release and allow your awareness to return to the moment.

THE PROCESS TO THIS POINT

1. Breathe
2. Ground and charge the body.
3. Set an intention if you choose.
4. Open and release along the midline current.

CHAPTER FIVE

THE CHAKRA SYSTEM

Next let's do a quick review of the chakra system. Most literature that you read will say that the chakras are separate and unique things in the body's auric/biofield field. Having had the fortune of being around many hospitals and clinics and watching people from before birth to after death, my definition of a chakra is different. Our bodies are governed by the same laws of physics that govern everything physical around you. Just as the auric field is made up of physical components like the gasses that your skin is releasing, the chakras are made from physical processes and are governed by the laws of physics.

Everyone has nerve endings in their body. Everyone has places in their body where nerve endings cluster. When you get a group of nerve endings together they are called a nerve plexus. No set of nerves fires in sequence in a plexus. For example: think of the nerves as forming a ring. The nerves at the top may fire first or they may fire third or they may not fire at all. The nerves at the bottom may fire once and stop for a while. The nerves at the side may fire second and then switch to firing continuously. This happens because nerves respond to stimulus.

Not all nerves in the body are firing all the time. So a nerve will fire and then stop and then start up again.

Nerves produce an electrical signal when they fire. Nerves carry electrical current from one part of the body to another. That electrical current stimulates the body to do things like move a muscle or let you know that you have been cut. All electricity produces a field. So the nerve that fires is producing an electrical field. It may not be a very big field but it does produce a field. This is just the basic physics of electricity. Because the nerves do not fire in a standard sequence and do not fire continuously, the electrical field that they produce when the nerves are clustered, wiggles. If there are enough nerve endings in one place, the field which is produced does not just wiggle but actually turns.

It is the firing of the nerve endings which produce the torsion and create the turning of electrical/electromagnetic field that is in turn called a "chakra."

Again, because the laws of physics apply to the body, the torsioned field moves magnetic and electric current into the body via the nerve plexus and out of the body via the turning field. All places where you have nerve endings come together and a torsioned field is created where the body communicates with the external environment.

Another way of saying "Chakra" is that it is an electromagnetic vortexes that feed nerve plexuses.

Your body responds to sound and light. And though you may not be able to hear it in a normal auditory range, the currents of light that are moving through your body have sounds too. With special equipment you can measure the sounds being created just as you can measure the frequency rate of the light wave. All waves of light carry information in the form of frequency, pitch, timber and tone. We do not always know how to interpret the information but it is present in the wave of light, the wave of current.

With the information we now have, it appears that different nerve plexuses generate and respond to different pitches of sound. The nerve plexus in the base of your pelvis is pitched differently than the one in your heart region and they are both different form the ones in your head.

The nerve plexus type, placement etc. controls the pitch, and the torsioned fields are in turn tuned by the pitch of the nerve plexus. Chakras, current flows that feed nerve groups in the body, work just as you use a tuner on your radio dial for 101.6 or 92.4. The chakra/electromagnetic vortex allows the body to tune to various frequencies and can draw off current or feed the body with those various frequencies.

There are a number of different nerve plexuses in the body. For each nerve plexus there is a chakra (torsioned and turning field). There are big or what could be called major chakras that feed nerve plexuses of twenty-one nerve endings or more. There are smaller or minor chakras that feed nerve plexuses of fourteen nerves or more, and then there are small chakras. There are over 100 nerve plexus/chakras combinations of various sizes in the body.

So these turning electromagnetic vortexes or chakras allow the body to be fed with energy/current/frequencies from the environment. These currents carry information. Imagine, if you will, that you are actually in a sea of energy and that sea of energy is constantly flowing in you, around you, and through you. The sea of energy, those frequencies of light and sound, are the flow that feeds and bathes each and every cell in the body. The electromagnetic vortexes/chakras are simply places which energy can move into and out of the body freely.

There are seven main nerve plexus/chakras that reside along the midline of the body. The first big chakra is between the two legs in the pelvic floor. The second chakra is in the pelvic region. The third feeds the solar plexus from just below it. The fourth is the heart area. The fifth resides in the throat. The sixth chakra is the third eye or the center of the forehead. And the seventh is the top of the head. Those are the largest chakras of the body. A common mistake in the understanding of many practitioners is that the chakras lie in a straight line up the body. In many people the nerve plexuses are slightly off to one side or another of the midline. This is why we check for still and stuck places in the midline current. It helps to allow the body to shift into a healthier configuration closer to having those plexuses in as straight a line as possible.

There are additional chakras on and off the body along which the current moves, starting in the ground and moving through the legs, adding in current from the first chakra region and being fed by all of the chakras as the current moves up the body flowing out through the top of the head and continuing up to the edge of the incarnational form. There are nerve plexus in your ankles, caves, knees, thighs and lots of places in between where you can find these additional chakras.

Along the midline and above the head outside of the body are the eighth, ninth and tenth chakras. These are structured differently for the vortexes on the body but they are still commonly called chakras. They don't feed nerve plexuses; they do spin but differently, and they do feed information into the midline current of the body on how you build your environment and how you build your life. I mention them so you are not surprised when you see them when you look at yourself in the mirror.

As we practice seeing, we are going to focus on two of these nerve plexuses/chakras. For the purposes of seeing auras, the sixth chakra, which encompasses the space just above the center point in the forehead and moves through the frontal lobe, the cortex, and goes all the way to the back of the head, and the seventh chakra, which is at the top of the head and top of the cortex, are the most important chakras/electromagnetic vortexes. The torsioned fields need to be turning fast enough in those areas to move sufficient current through the area to stimulate the pineal and pituitary.

Think of a chakra/electromagnetic vortex as a mini flattened sort of tornado. It looks a lot like one. For example: think of the way a whirlpool in water spins downward like a gigantic V. Inside this spinning field are actually a number of smaller spinning areas based on how often each of the various nerve are firing. They are all working together, which make up the larger field flow. Often in esoteric literature the chakras will be described as flowers or lotus blossoms with many petals. In my experience, the nerve plexuses/chakras that are firing and turning and actually look more like lotus blossoms, are chakras of people who are substantially farther down the path of enlightenment.

PLACEMENT OF THE "BIG" NERVE PLEXUS/CHAKRAS

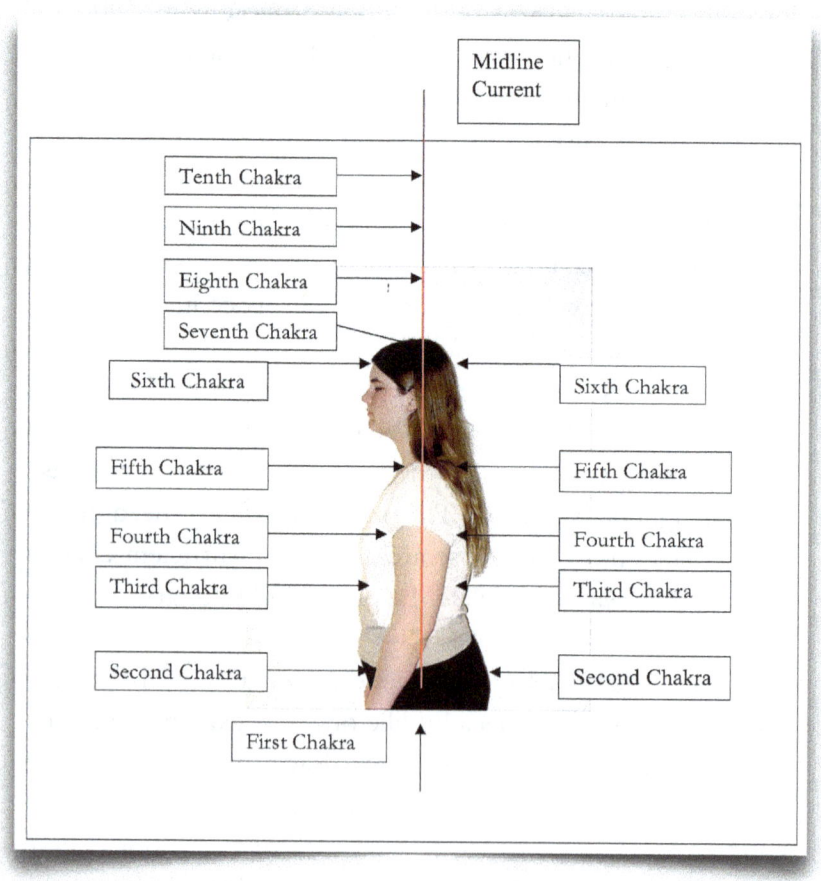

Let's take a moment to discuss another piece of the chakra structure. Each chakra, as I have mentioned before, looks something like a tornado and there is a lid-type charge that acts as a cover of any chakra. This cover is produced by a change in the tension on the surface of the electrical field. Any electrical field in the body of any size has a magnetic component.

Thunderstorm cloud form which looks like a Chakra field.
May 17, 2009 Marana, AZ

This magnetic charge is strong at the top of the vortex and acts as a cover and a filter. It acts to screen the amount of current, and the frequency range of the current which the torsioned fields may take in from the environment around them. With time and training a person begins to be able to pick and choose what information to receive and what information to leave out. Over time as more current flows through the cover of the chakra/vortex it becomes more and more transparent and flexible.

Remember these fields are made of light and light frequency, which has information. For those people who are substantially farther down the path of enlightenment the covering, or protection, of the chakra is not present in the same way. The chakra cover becomes thinner, more transparent and flexible; the torsioned field has a tendency to blossom out more fully. Rather than having a flat top it has more of a curved shape, thus appearing more like the petals on a flower.

In order to see your field or someone else's field fully it is best to have all of the electromagnetic vortexes/chakras flowing and spinning. This means that your nerve plexus has to be functioning and stimulated. You can stimulate a nerve plexus by poking it, by focusing your attention on it, by setting an intention and by breathing into it.

If you have lived on Earth you have issues and memories. Because memory is stored in the waters of the body, and the body is held together by water, most people have issues that are stored in the water of their cells. Nerve cells are held together by water molecules just like any other cells. Because of this "issue" retention it's less likely that all of the nerve cells are functioning fully. Less nerve function results in less spin, less current available, less freedom to get the current to the correct spot in the body, which results in less of an ability to see. Focusing on a particular nerve plexus and its chakra field is an important step to creating sufficient current flow. Clearing stuck places, blocked places, from your tissues initiates that process.

It is important to clear overcharge out of the vortexes too. In the way that you can get static on a phone, you can get static in the charged field of the chakra. Think of the way that you might have rubbed a balloon on your clothes and then stuck the balloon on the wall, when you were a kid. In a very similar way information can get stuck in the field that is the chakra. In particular the tips and the covers are vulnerable. It is important that the tips of the chakra, the very ends, where it seats into the midline power current, be as open, clear, and flexible as possible.

If there is energy that is stuck in the tip of the chakra, because of a water-held memory in the cells, that is too tender to touch in on, the flow through the chakra/vortex will not be complete. Nor will it be able to transmit the necessary information you would like to have flowing and available to you. Remember, electricity flows along the path of least resistance. If there is resistance in the field the current will not flow as it should. As we practice this next meditation lesson, consider the flexibility of the chakra cover, the clearing of all these tornado-like vortexes and their tip ends. You will want to assure that there are no blocks/stuck areas in the middle of the stream, thereby enabling the current to run smoothly, quickly, and fully through the chakra/vortex and into the body.

To make sure that the electromagnetic vortex/chakra is moving fast enough, we will use a combination of imagination, intention and focus. Take the thumb of your right hand and touch it to your forehead in the center just above the midpoint between your hair line and your eyebrows. Put the thumb in facing into your forehead.

Curve the fingers of your right hand over as if you're closing your hand. Now, turn your hand and follow your fingers around. That's the direction, counterclockwise, that the front of the chakra turns when you are north of the equator.

MEDITATION TO OPEN FLOW IN 6TH CHAKRA

Visualize the chakra, the tornado turning. Imagine that it's turning reasonably, at approximately the speed that a second hand on a stop watch would make with one sixty-second cycle. Envision your vortexes spinning at this rate of speed, then imagine them spinning faster, making the second hand sweep around in thirty seconds, then in ten. See any stuck places spinning out of the chakra as it turns. Can you feel the flow of current moving physically through your tissue? If not, spend time breathing into the area of the nerve plexus and visualizing the vortex that is the chakra turning and moving freely.

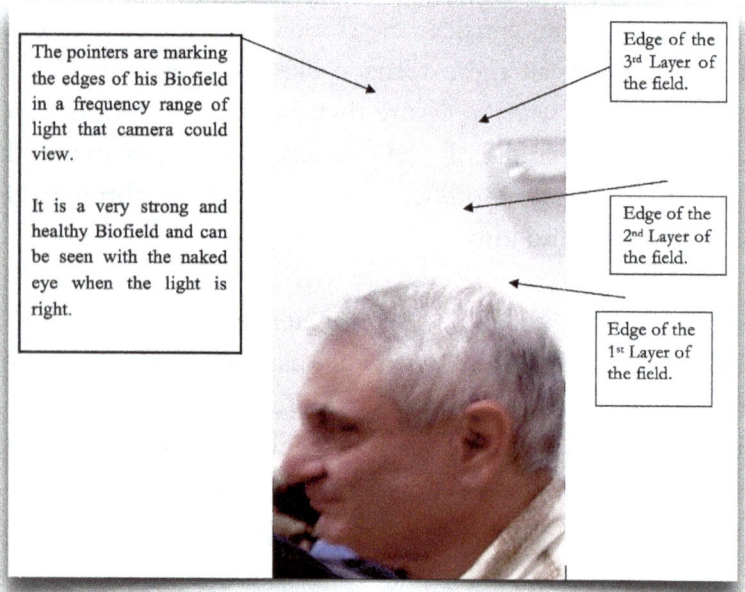

Next set your intention to have all your nerve plexuses in the body working in a healthy fashion. Set your intention to have the current moving freely in and out of each and every nerve plexus in the body. You can repeat this process with the 7th chakra too.

Meditation to clear the tips of the 6th and 7th Chakras

Begin to focus on the tips of the vortexes of the 6th and 7th chakras where they seat into the midline current at the top of the head. See how well you can feel the flow of current into the area. See if you can feel the current moving all the way from the front to the back of your head. Any place you cannot feel the current moving, focus. Breathe into that spot. And just watch it until it moves and current moves freely again.

Meditation to increase spin in 6th Chakra

The next step is to make sure that once the vortexes are open, they are spinning fast enough to generate enough current flow to the correct area. Imagine the tornadoes turning both front and back with their tips meeting in the middle of your head. Allow yourself to imagine a river flowing in and then flowing back out on a separate current, filling a lake and flowing back out. Allow yourself to imagine that this river and the tornado can move faster and faster, but with even flow, so if the river moves faster in, it also moves faster out. If the tornado, the flow of current, spins faster, the river moves faster in and faster out, bathing the area, but not staying and stagnating in the area. You need to have this river moving in and out, the tornado spinning faster and faster, to properly cleanse the area. Everything should have a smooth and consistent flow, and also be moving at about the same speed. This will fill the area with energy.

Allow yourself to see a consistent flow of energy through the area. If it starts to feel as if you're getting a headache, stop. You are overcharging the area, and you are not allowing the energy to flow back out. Set an intention to clear the area again. Spend some time focusing on any place that is stuck. Give yourself time to breathe and relax again. Then when you begin using your tool of imagination again, be sure that you allow yourself to focus on the energy going out equally to the energy coming in. A consistent and smooth flow is extremely important.

Once you feel you can allow a smooth inflow and outflow through the front and the back of the sixth chakra, allow yourself to see how fast you can get the tornadoes to spin. Do it for a few seconds at a time. Never do it to the point of discomfort. This should be a comfortable and easy process. If you are experiencing discomfort, stop. Relax a bit and then practice the meditation again, clearing those blocks, straightening the current and opening up the flow. This may take several attempts, so don't force the process if the pain persists. Relax and try again later.

6th and 7th Chakra T-junction at Pineal and Pituitary

MEDITATION TO INCREASE FLOW IN THE 7TH CHAKRA

When you are ready, begin to work with the seventh chakra, the chakra on the top of the head. Again, allow a smooth flow of current to come into the chakra and out of the chakra. Allow the energy to flow in through the chakra down the midline power current and also allow the energy from the midline power current to squirt back out the top of the head.

Allow the energy to move fully and freely as the electromagnetic vortex/chakra turns. Envision how the chakra would look as it is spinning clockwise. What would each of the individual tornadoes look like spinning? How fast would they be spinning?

Then allow yourself a conscious connection to how it feels. Once you can feel the chakra turning, allow the feeling of the energy moving in the chakra and out of the chakra as it spins at the same time.

COMBINE 6TH AND 7TH CHAKRAS

When you're ready, envision the feeling of the energy of the chakra coming in and out of the sixth chakra and the energy coming in and out of the seventh chakra at the same time. Practice this for several days, until you have a clear awareness of the energy moving in and out of the sixth chakra and in and out of the seventh. You'll know you are ready to proceed by the change in temperature to this region, when the current's flow becomes cool. My daughter says it feels like her fans are turning. It will be a very similar experience to having a cool breeze blowing all about your head. This is when you'll have succeeded in maintaining a consistent and synchronized flow of current throughout the sixth and seventh chakras.

MEDITATION ON THE COVERS CHAKRA SYSTEM

Once you can feel chakras 6 and 7 working together, begin to attempt to see the energy moving up the midline power current. See what it feels like. How does it feel when the energy flows up the current and mixes in with the flows going in and out of the chakras?

One of the things you can do to increase the flow of energy in and out of the chakras is to focus on the covers and on the tips of each of the chakras. For example, to make the covers more flexible, imagine that you are taking your thumb and pushing it on the lid of your plastic lunch container. It gives a little and then releases when you release your thumb. Again, using your imagination as a tool, focus on the chakra cover moving in and out as if there is a thumb pushing against a piece of plastic, and then release it and watch it stretch back out. Move it forward and back, gently. Do this about ten times at a sitting and then take a break.

Then focus on the tips of the chakra in order starting with the first and moving up the body. Imagine the center of the tips moving in and out the same way, as if they're being hit by a mallet on a drum, flexing as they give, and then releasing. Watch them giving and releasing, giving and releasing, stretching and releasing back and forth. This practice of stretching and releasing allows the tips and the cover to become more flexible. When the tips and the cover of the chakra are more flexible, more energy can move across it more freely.

Spend the time that you need practicing the material in this section. There is no substitute for clearing so that the field moves freely. You may have spent years letting the field be still. You may have let things move more slowly so that you did not have to see. But to start to see again you must get the correct amount of current to the correct spot in the body. So spend the time and get a free and open flow of current started!

QUICK RECAP ~ CHAKRA FLOW

1. Breathe.
2. Ground and charge.
3. Set and intention if you choose.
4. Breathe into the midline current and allow any tension to dissolve away.
5. Allow the current to move freely up and down the midline.
6. Feel into each of the large nerve plexus in order beginning with the base of the pelvis.
7. Allow all tension in each of the areas of the nerve plexus to dissolve away.
8. Just watch as a free flow of current starts to move through each of the nerve plexus.
9. Breathe into each of the nerve plexus beginning with the base of the pelvis.
10. Enjoy the feeling of the "cool breeze" that begins to flow through your body!

CHAPTER SIX

CLEARING THE NOISE

Remember when we mentioned allowing the energy to go up and down the midline power current and to wash away all the stuck places/ blocks that were in the middle of the current? Well, very often you have to do the same thing with the sixth and seventh chakras. These chakras can have a very specific type of block impeding the current flow. This block is known as a "veil." The veil is like a screen you cannot really see through, thin and somewhat flexible, almost translucent. We want to clear the veil-like structures away. The veils are often very old blocks or places with static charge that just have not quite dissolved away. A very good way of washing those veils away is to allow your connection to God, Source, the divine, all that is, your "Higher Power" (however you would prefer to describe it), to bring in love energy, and wash through the sixth and seventh chakras. The following meditation exercise will help in clearing away the veils.

MEDITATION TO CLEAR THE NOISE

Allow yourself to breathe. Breathe in for four, pause for one, and exhale for four. When you've done three good breaths, allow the mind to focus. Allow yourself to connect to the current flow in whatever way you normally connect. Connect in whatever way you relate to and connect with the life force that permeates and surrounds our bodies and all that exists.

Allow yourself to have a current of energy moving from above your head into the top of your head. Focus on how that current feels moving in and out of your physical body. Imagine that a current of white light is present and the white light begins to flow like water. Set an intention to be able to feel the current of white light. Breathe. Imagine the white light is pouring into the top of your head. With that white light, all the veils in the current dissolve. See if you can feel the veils dissolving and the change in pressure in your head as a result. Set an intention that the veils dissolve fully and completely. Breathe. Watch as the water from the stream of white light washes out through the front and back of the sixth chakra, spilling over the body. It washes down the midline power current. Allow yourself to feel the love of all as the current pours through the top of your head, washing out the area, dissolving all the veils. It is dissolving everything out of the way so healthy current can move freely.

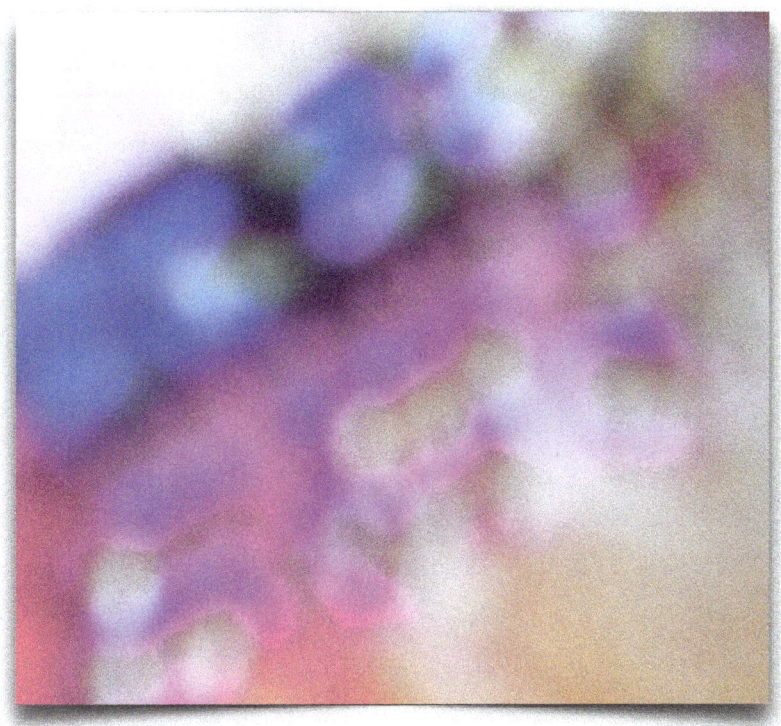

This is similar to the way the current flow looks as it moves through the veils.

Imagine that the universe is giving you this flow of current as a gift to you. Imagine that you can feel the emotion of the current as well, the pure love that comes with the current. Then attempt to really perceive it. See if you can allow yourself to feel the love that the universe feels for you, in this moment. And breathe.

Allow these veils to be washed away in the energy that is pouring through your head. It dissolves away all of the blocks, all of the veils that are in the way.

When it feels as if you have smooth flow and all of the blocks and veils have been dissolved, allow yourself a moment of thanks and gratitude for the support in this time space now.

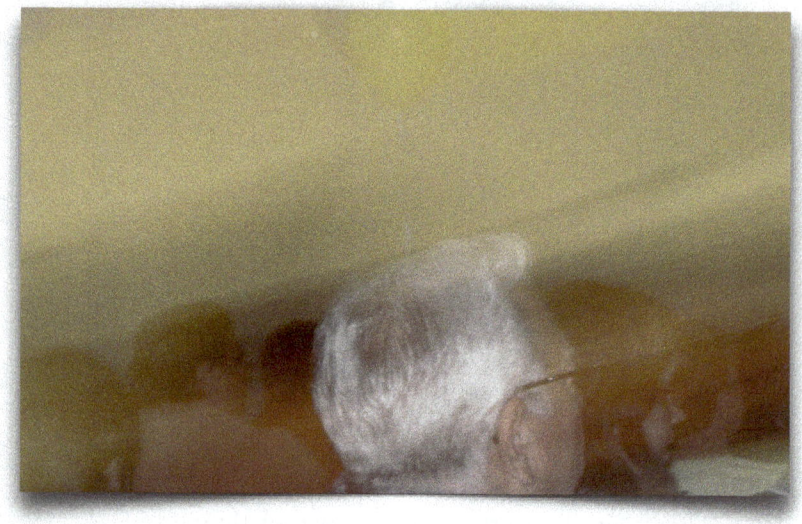

We live in a sea of energy. This is an example of some of the current flow that abounds in our everyday environment.

CHAPTER SEVEN

ARCS OF LIGHT

Once you have basic current flow established in the body and have flow moving freely through the sixth and seventh chakras, you are ready to begin seeing the field. Because most adults run a much less active field than a child, you may want to add an additional source of light to help power the process. The pineal and pituitary glands have to receive sufficient stimulation to trigger the release of hormones that will in turn stimulate the nerve plexus which open your visual system to a new frequency range. Though I believe this way of seeing is an older visual system in terms of human evolution, it will be a "new" way of seeing for you at this time.

To add that last little bit of raw power, you may want to add arcs of light to your energy flow to help stimulate the pineal and pituitary glands and allow the third eye to open and see more fully. It is not necessary to always run these arches of light, but in the beginning it does aid the seeing, and I often suggest that people use it to increase the clarity and accuracy when seeing at a more advanced stage.

MEDITATION TO STIMULATE THE PINEAL AND PITUITARY

Imagine if you will, a gold arch of light coming from the first chakra, which is located between your legs, and curving like a gigantic letter C, moving into your forehead. Imagine that this current is three or four inches across, deep, and wide. It's a round current and flows fully from the front of the first chakra curving up and going in the front of the sixth. Now set an intention to have that current flow manifest. Then focus on the area and see if you can feel the current moving from the first chakra, moving through your field and coming into the forehead area. And breathe!

Placement of the Arcs of Light

Now imagine that there is a current of rose light coming out of the tip of your tailbone. In this case, the rose light flows out of the tailbone and makes a big vertical curve up across the torso and comes in the back of head in the sixth chakra. It is as if your back is the straight line in a D and the light makes the curve. Now set an intention to have that current flow manifest. Then focus on the area and see if you can feel the current moving from the tail bone, moving through your field and coming into the back of the head. And breathe!

Allow yourself to imagine a gold arc in front and a matching rose arc in back. Feel the two arcs moving through your field. Allow yourself to imagine those two arcs of light mixing in the head, in the pineal and pituitary glands and stimulating them, just as if you were running fingers up a keyboard listening to the scale. These glands are located almost in the center of your brain but are slightly offset behind the center.

TAKE A LOOK! When you feel that you can coordinate all of these things, then allow yourself to hold your hand up in front of the body. It's useful to have a room that is very slightly dimmed, or a white wall to look against. If you are seeing just your physical hand, then allow yourself to increase the amount of flow of energy through the body. Draw more energy through the feet. Allow the sixth and seventh chakras to spin faster. Don't close your eyes. Do blink your eyes. Do allow your gaze to soften slightly, and breathe. The breath is the fire, the breath is the flow, and the breath generates the current that allows you to see.

This is similar to what you can see as you begin to restore your ability to see the field. As you look at the edge of your hand it may appear as shimmers, blue or a bit cloudy. There will be a thin edge around your hand. It will vary from about a ¼ inch to about 2 inches in width.

Over time you will begin to see structures in the fluid layers of the field. In the beginning of that process they may look a bit like ripples.

QUICK RECAP ~ ARCS OF LIGHT

1. Breathe.
2. Ground, putting your feet in the iron core in the center of the Earth, allowing yourself to receive the energy back into the body.
3. Set an intention if you choose.
4. Allow the midline power current to have smooth energy flow, and the energy moves up the midline power current.
5. Focus on the energy to flow in and out of the sixth and seventh chakras. Make sure it is moving smoothly and easily.
6. Have the chakras spin faster than they perhaps ordinarily would.
7. Add a gold-colored current of energy to come out the front of the first chakra into the front of the sixth chakra, a rose-colored current to come out of the back of the first chakra at the tailbone, and into the back of the sixth chakra.
8. Allow those two currents to mix and stimulate the pineal and pituitary glands.
9. Relax the physical eyes, blink regularly, and see what you see.
10. Repeat this several times.

CHAPTER EIGHT

LOOKING THROUGH THE FOREHEAD

Gradually, as you allow sufficient current, you'll begin to see the shimmer around a physical hand. One of the things that can help you see this initial shimmer is to practice "switching up" to looking through your forehead. Remember we are not using the physical eye's visual system except to mix the information. To see the field we have to look in a different set of frequencies that are processed in what I believe is a historically older visual system. So we are "switching up" into looking though the nerve plexuses that are in the brain.

MEDITATION FOR "SWITCHING UP"

To practice this switch of looking through the forehead, first do it with your eyes open. Feel into how your forehead feels at the same time. Can you feel the cool breeze of your turning chakra? Then feel again your physical eyes. Can you feel the difference in the placement of each in your head? Now practice with your eyes closed. Feel your physical eyes. Feel your forehead, or even what it feels like inside your head just behind the forehead. Now practice moving between those two sensate experiences. Go up and down three or four times in a row. Then keep the feeling of the forehead present.

Look out of your eyes, then close your eyes, and allow yourself to feel as if you're looking out of your forehead. While you're in that viewing state of looking out of your forehead, open your eyes. Keep the feeling of looking out of your forehead. Allow the consciousness of your mind to be in your forehead, just the same way that we moved the consciousness throughout the physical body to clear the midline power current. What kind of colors are you seeing? What kind of images? You may start to get lots of shapes and colors as you do this exercise.

Now relax your eyes and release the feeling of looking through your forehead. In a moment we will try it again. Check in with yourself. Did you feel tension around your eyes, your jaw, your neck, or your shoulders? If so, then relax these muscle groups and breathe into those various areas. Then begin to practice again. Open the eyes, look through the eyes, and really look through them. Do not just look the way you would in everyday life. Find something to focus on and actively take in the details about it. Then close your eyes and look through the forehead. Allow yourself to feel your vision shift upward. See if you have images or colors, shapes or flows coming through.

Then focus, looking through the forehead, and open the eyes back up. Hold that position for a few seconds, now breathe, release, and breathe again. Do not hyperventilate. Breathe gently. Now release the feeling of the forehead. You may want to practice this process a number of times, so that you can open the eyes and look and still have the feeling of seeing through the forehead comfortably. You'll find that as you do this, it becomes easier to switch up, so that you reach a point where you don't have to close the eyes before you add the feeling of looking through the forehead.

When you begin to look through the forehead, you may see afterimages when you open your eyes. That means that you are in fact increasing the flow across the sixth and seventh chakras and stimulating the third eye region. That's a good step, and you're making fine progress.

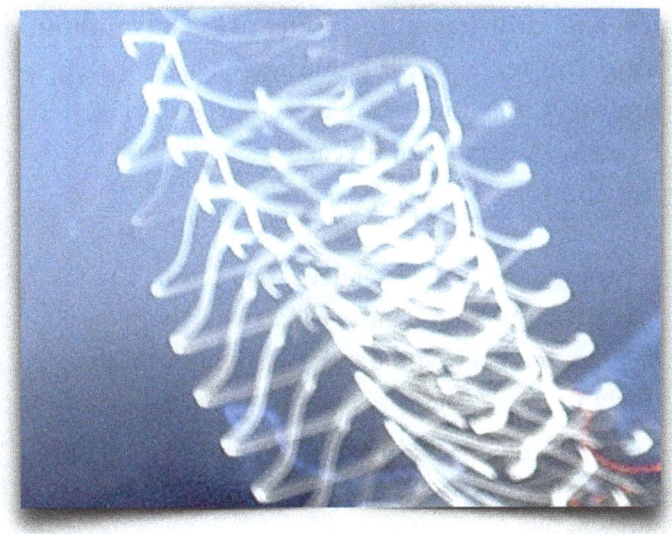

Similar to the way a light pulse looks as it travels along the vertebrae of the spine.

You will want to consider practicing this process whenever you have a moment that is quiet. Do it for a couple of minutes at a time and several times a day. Remember to blink whenever your physical eyes are open. We are not looking for an after-image. We are looking to develop a change in perception so that another set of frequencies that the body is receiving can be perceived accurately and interpreted correctly.

A CAUTION!

In the beginning of this practice many students will get colors and shapes from the first moment. Some will not and will only get small shimmers. Be where you are. Let the growth in your ability to see happen gradually and gently so that you can incorporate the change without stress. **If you are feeling any kind of discomfort go back to the basics and drill grounding, clearing the midline and clearing the 6th and 7th chakras.** There should be no discomfort if this process is done correctly. Do not push your body; instead, drill each section until you are comfortable.

This process requires practice time each day. A small amount of practice over time allows your body to adjust to the changes gradually and gently. Do not push. Practice, get comfortable with the process and let the vision open naturally and gently. Remember to breathe and have fun! You are on a voyage to experience your body and the world around you in a lovely way.

While you practice remember to keep relaxing. Check your shoulders. Check your neck. Are they feeling tight? If so, do some gentle stretching exercises. Remember to breathe. Current flows in waves. For many people that means in the beginning they will see for just an instant. Do not push when that happens; instead, relax more fully, let the flow of current increase and you will see again. If you stop breathing or hold your breath it will lessen your ability to see as the wave rises again. Just relax and enjoy.

QUICK RECAP ~ SWITCHING UP

1. Breathe.
2. Practice first with your eyes open.
3. Feel into how your forehead feels at the same time. Can you feel the cool breeze of your turning chakra?
4. Then feel again your physical eyes. Can you feel the difference in the placement of each in your head?
5. Now practice with your eyes closed. Feel your physical eyes.
6. Feel your forehead, or even what it feels like inside your head just behind the forehead.
7. Now practice moving between those two sensate experiences. Up and down three or four times in a row. Then keep the feeling of the forehead present.
8. Then open and look out of your physical eyes.
9. Now close your eyes, and allow yourself to feel as if you're looking out of your forehead.
10. While you're in that viewing state of looking out of your forehead, open your eyes back up. Keep the feeling of looking out of your forehead.
11. Practice and repeat several times.
12. Allow yourself to feel your vision shift upward.
13. See if you have images, colors, or shapes coming through.

CHAPTER NINE

STAGES OF SEEING

Let's talk for a moment about how auric vision seems to re-establish in a person. Most people imagine that they can go from not seeing the auric field to seeing a full auric field instantly, as if something magical happens. It probably took several years for your ability to see to turn off, so you may want to consider giving yourself more time. And sometimes when people have been taught the process of seeing, it does happen fast, but not often. Often people can see shimmers within a day, but for more complete seeing it can take more time. For many people, it takes practice, and you practice each step by:

- Breathing
- Grounding
- Intention setting if you choose.
- Charging and clearing the midline power current.
- Spinning your chakras faster, being aware of those chakras.
- Clearing the veils.
- Running the arcs of light to stimulate the pineal and pituitary regions.
- Looking through your forehead.
- Allowing yourself to see and perceive.

Most people learn to see the aura in stages. The first thing that often happens is they begin to see shimmers around the objects they are looking at, kind of like the way a runway looks on a hot day, or a road on a hot day when the heat shimmers off of it.

Gradually over time, the shimmer takes on a white or opal quality to it as your power curve increases. Once you begin to get a white quality to the shimmer, you may start to actually see a crisp edge line to the shimmer. Look at how far out the shimmer goes from the actual object that it's surrounding, and how close in. Some people will see the edges around the object, but not the field on the surface of the object, at least not initially.

As your power curve increases and there is a more powerful flow stimulating the sixth chakra (third eye region), you'll begin to see color come in. This is the place where most people begin to develop discernment as to what colors mean in the field. There are several very fine books available today on the meanings of colors in the auric field. They all present good theories and some present good experimental practice. You might want to explore learning more about what the different colors mean as you begin to see color.

Another thing that happens at this stage is people begin to move into one model of seeing or another. The most common of these models are the "unified auric field" model and the "layered auric field" model. No one way of seeing the field is more right than any other. It may be that there are as many ways to see the field, as there are people to see it. Humans are works of art. Each one is individual and unique.

However, we are going to focus on these two ways of perceiving the field because they are very common ways of seeing.

The unified auric field model postulates that there is one large field that resembles a sort of egg shaped ball around the body. In this model the auric field is multi-colored and flowing. The layered field model suggests that the field is flowing on some layers and structured on others.

In my experience perceiving the field as unified is a function of power current level and placement of that current. When a person has sufficient power current, one actually sees layering to the field, not just one field with lots of different colors. Also my experience has shown that most people who see the field with many different colors and no structures are either looking at just the frequencies of the second layer of the field or just the frequencies of the fourth layer of the field, which are both fluid colored layers.

This is not wrong. It is not a bad thing to observe people from the frequency range of the heart. It is just one way of seeing and perceiving. As the power current increases, my students seem to develop more discernment, and accuracy, and be able see layers within the auric field.

Similar to the way the lines of light look from a distance on the 7th layer.

The layers I perceive and the form I perceive that they take are listed below. Each layer seems to resonate within a specific frequency set and range. Thus it carries specific types of information that are held in the light in that frequency range. Remember that you are a work of art and will perceive in the way that is correct for you. Everything that you see in the field is simply more information, in the same way as what a person is wearing gives you information. In the way in which I see, there are colored structured layers/frequency sets that have actual form with a distinctive grid pattern for each layer. They seem to be woven of thought and are the resonances of the weak Van de Wals forces that hold the water molecules of the body together. There are also layers/frequency sets with more complexity, which are fluid and cloud like. Those seem to store memory, emotion, and trauma, often in an image based form. A brief description of the ten auric layers which I perceive as being inside the person's incarnational form is below:

- The first layer of the field is usually a steel grey blue to a cobalt blue, and it's a structured grid layer. It is often woven of thoughts about physical safety.
- The second layer is a fluid cloud layer. It often contains images and emotions that tie into the sensate and sensual experience of the body.
- The third layer is a lemon-yellow structured grid layer. It is again woven of thought and focuses on hunger, survival, and how you are perceived by yourself and others.
- The fourth layer is another fluid cloud layer, but it's paler, and less dense, more like loosely set Jell-O, or green Slime that you'd buy at the store for children. This layer seems to focus on many of our emotional reactions like love, anger, sorrow, and joy. In my experience many of our emotional traumas are stored on this layer, and with a small charge put into the area which stores the memory, you can watch it replay like watching a video tape.
- The fifth layer is often a white layer of threads on a blue background, close to a sky-blue color, and is a structured grid layer. Thoughts of honor and truth, and the voice that you bring to your life can be found on this layer.
- The sixth layer is a fluid cloud layer; it is iridescent with a shimmering effect, much like the semiprecious stone opal, or mother of pearl found in abalone shells. All of the colors of the sixth layer which I have seen have a lovely pearly quality. This layer is about vision and what we allow ourselves to see and perceive. Many of the images

have aspects of spirituality and our place in the order of things.
- The seventh layer of the field is a true gold that ranges from a burnished gold to a very bright gold and is a structured grid layer. Again woven of thought, it often holds the learning of a spiritual nature.
- The eighth and tenth layers of the field are both fluid cloud layers, becoming brighter, shinier, with the colors more and more transparent, less dense, and the fluids more flowing as you move higher in frequency. The eighth layer seems to store images of integration. Those images of insight and moments when we perceive the larger nature of our actions in relationship to others. The tenth layer appears to me to have a direct connection to all that is around us. It seems to hold images of us when we are the most connected and in truth to all that is.
- The ninth layer of the field is a platinum colored structured grid layer. It appears to connect to the altruistic acts which we think about and do.

One of the things that you may want to practice as you learn more about the colors and images of the auric field is aligning yourself to one level or another, so that you can clearly discern which layer you are looking at and what is in the auric field layer. Be sure that you are able to perceive clear colors in the field before you begin to practice adjusting for different layers/frequency sets.

Once you have clear colors in the field, then you can specifically tune your field to perceiving different layers. To tune your seeing, pick a strong corresponding sense. For example, you would use your sense of smell, your kinesthetic sense, or your sense of hearing. Using the kinesthetic sense to tune, you would feel into the area of the chakra in your own body, which would correspond to the area where you want to look. For example, to tune yourself to the second layer of the auric field, feel your pelvic area, then allow the sensation of your pelvis to spill up your body as if were a fountain flowing upward.

Or you can hear the sound that your pelvis makes; tune to that sound and allow that sound to resonate in the 6th chakra region and then look at the other person's second layer. You can also tune yourself to the taste or smell of your second chakra and view another's second layer. All of the senses will work if you tune in fully to your chakra, and then bring that set of frequencies to the 6th chakra.

If you wish to see this layer on another person then you must also connect to the layer of another person's field. Your chakra and the other person's chakras act as a bell note for the field layer. For example, my fourth chakra is pitched at the G above middle C. That is the bell note, the midpoint of the auditory frequencies for that field layer. It is the defining note (G above middle C) for the fourth layer of my field. Pitches may vary slightly from one person to another. So can the taste and smell, but there will be a regular and consistent pattern that you will be able to identify in your own field which you can use as a spring board to connect to the other person's field and pitches.

Similar to looking at structured layers of the field. As if you are looking downward to the current flows of the layer below.

In addition, it's also possible to see more than one layer at one time. You can see a number of different layers around yourself or the person that you are looking at simply by having all of the large chakras open and spinning at one time. This brings a full current up the midline power current and allows the sixth chakra to open and spin very solidly. With all of those frequency sets flowing into the region of the 6th chakra, all of that lovely light/information/frequency comes along and it allows you to see lots of information. It may sound overwhelming, but remember, seeing that fully usually comes with time. As I mentioned before, most people begin by seeing a shimmer effect, and then move to seeing a white or cloud like shimmer, gradually filling in color as the power current increases and the stimulation of the third eye region increases.

Give yourself the opportunity to really connect and explore the field. There is nothing to be afraid of and it is a tremendously joyous process beginning this journey of discovery. Always fun, always exciting, it's never the same from moment to moment; where there is a color one day does not necessarily mean there will be a color there the next. Look, explore, and enjoy!

Similar to the way the lines of light look in the field after there is a percussive blow to the body. The result on the physical body would be a bruise.

REVIEW ~ STAGES OF SEEING

1. Shimmery field around the edges of the body. (Much like the waves on a hot road.)
2. White cloudy film around the body.
3. Bright blue spark zipping around the edge of the body.
4. White film gets a blue or yellow tint.
5. Shadows having color tints.
6. Thin films of color passing over the body.
7. Color density increases.
8. Lines of light in a grid form over the surface of the body.
9. Different colored lines of light and the ability to see how far they extend past the surface of the body.
10. Colored flows moving over the lines of light.
11. Clear chakra structures.
12. Clear images of people, situations or objects.
13. Video tapes of the clients experiences playing in the field.

CHAPTER TEN

OBSTACLES OF SEEING

Let's take a moment and look at some of the obstacles to seeing the auric field.

THE FEAR OF SEEING THE AURIC FIELD

The first and most common obstacle is fear. Many people become uncomfortable or scared with just the thought of seeing the auric field. They are afraid of what they're going to see. I suggest that you use your imagination as a tool toward resolving your fear. What is the most awful thing that you can imagine seeing in the auric field? What is totally yucky, scary and horrid? Do it, imagine your fears. You may want to make a list of several things (perhaps a top ten list) that are really yucky in your imagination and that you're afraid to see. Guess what! When you have imagined them you have looked at them. Thus you have already "seen" the very worst that you can see in the field. Then acknowledge that since you've already imagined them, there really isn't any need to be concerned. You have seen them and there is nothing worse to see. Now that you've imagined them, look at your fears and they won't be such a big deal.

Another way to diminish your fears is after reviewing your list of worst things, make a top ten list of the best things you could see in a person's field. Perhaps it is the fact that some special person loves you or that their energy is flowing freely. It could be that their field is very clear, bright and joyous. You could see an experience in the field that is filled with laughter, perhaps even a memory that was shared by you and this person. Remember, as your power current increases in the body you will be able to see memories like that, just as if you're watching a video on TV.

This is similar to the way a negative thought form can look in the field. It is just noise. It is not in truth.
Why be afraid of static?

THE POTENTIAL ABUSE OF POWER

The next obstacle to seeing is often linked to the abuse of power, or concern about the abuse of power involved with using what you would be seeing. Many people have some level of fear of this because they feel if they see something in someone's auric field they must take action on it. It is not a requirement that when you see something you must do something about it. And in fact, in the next section, we'll discuss the ethics of what you do when you see something unexpected in the field. Generally, what you will be seeing in the field you will simply mark down to yourself as just more information. You will not take any action based on what you see.

If you are really concerned about abusing the power of seeing things in people's fields, allow yourself to test various scenarios as your vision comes in. What are the kinds of situations that may come up where you might abuse the power of seeing in the field? Think about it carefully, because if you have a fear that you will abuse the power, undoubtedly some situation will come up to test you on this issue.

Since that's often the case, it's always wise to be prepared. Think about it carefully. In this situation, what would I do? Then begin to test yourself in day-to-day life. Ask, if I look at the field at any moment, and see one of the fears on my list, what would I do? Then practice with what you decide. Most often my students develop a set of patterns they understand that would help them deal with various situations in their life and make them feel uncomfortable. Once they develop an active plan, they lose their sense of discomfort, and gradually their auric vision comes in more fully.

Let me give you an example. While in a staff meeting one day, I was observing an interaction between two coworkers; during this interaction I realized that the two people were involved with one another. I could have abused the situation and given the information to others in the office, thereby causing trouble for them. I could have gone to either person and said, I am aware of your personal involvement with one another, which could have also caused difficulties for them. Instead I kept my own counsel. The people went on about their business as I went on about mine, and things flowed smoothly and serenely. Not long afterward, I noticed these two were no longer in a relationship. The situation had ended during the normal course of life events, and needed no interference or input from me. This is a fine example of noninterference after considering a situation, how information comes to us, and how my wise choice in this matter was best for all parties involved. Discernment and careful conscience searching before any action on your part is a required responsibility associated with seeing information in the field.

They Think I Am Different!

The next most common obstacle to seeing is being afraid that people will think you are different, or that people will become scared because you can see something that they can't see. Simply because you can see something in the auric field does not mean that you have to act on it, discuss it ever, or that you have to talk about the fact that you can see in every circumstance that you are in. You can pick and choose with whom and when you discuss that you can see the field. In most cases, what you're actually seeing should not be shared with anyone except the person that you're seeing it around. More than that, you should share it with that person only under very specific circumstances. The information is yours, and it does not necessarily have to be public. The fact that you can see the field does not have to be public. Pick and choose with whom you would discuss the fact that you're seeing the auric field. If your Aunty Mazy doesn't believe in seeing the auric field, and might be frightened by it, she is probably not the best person with whom to discuss the fact that you're seeing the second layer of the field.

"But I Just Had to Tell Them!"

It is not uncommon for my students to confide that they felt they had to reveal to a person what they had seen in that person's field. As a sound and general rule, if you feel you have to tell the person what you saw, don't! This obstacle to seeing is a subtle test we place in front of ourselves, the test of self-control and confidentiality. If you get a compelling feeling to confide what you have seen of that person's field, stop yourself. Wait as long as it takes for the need to reveal this information to subside. Once that wave passes, then you can clearly discern what you would gain from the process and what the other person would gain. Ask yourself if the information is something that they really need to know. How will this information be responded to? When you are in the state of feeling compelled to inform, you are not in the proper mindset and heart focus to exercise discernment and adequate judgment. The information would not be passed along in a cohesive and clear, nonjudgmental manner, but would be cluttered with some of your own personal issues.

Remember, people can be seriously challenged by the information you might provide them. Be gentle and compassionate, be thoughtful and wise, and above all don't share the information unless they request it. Keep your own counsel; be very sure you understand what you gain from sharing information with another before you do so, if at all. Information is power. Abuse of information only gives you power in the short term. And the back lash can be nasty. Follow the general rule: Do they absolutely need to know?

No, I Don't Want To

The next obstacle to seeing is the, "No, I don't want to" attitude. This stems from our childhood, while growing up we were all faced with something we just did not want to do. It was often something that someone, generally older, expected or demanded us to do. The outcome of these childhood experiences is that we created a place where we hold this energy in the body that is still saying "no!"

Sometimes that energy is located along the midline power current or in the head. Sometimes the energy is in the hips or the tummy. It is major block when it is in those areas, and because of that it changes the flow of current through the body, bending and twisting the current off the body's midline. Or the energy may get stuck when coming into the sixth or seventh chakra region, so there is no flow into that region. These blocks prevent the seeing process.

To remedy this problem I suggest that students engage their powerful "no" by giving themselves the chance to express it. This could be while you are alone. You could practice making contact with that space in your body and yelling out "No!" Or you might take a tennis racquet and bashing a pile of pillows while saying "no," thereby giving the body and the energy system permission to say the "no" that has been held on to for so long. Once the "no" has been expressed verbally, most of the time the energy block will clear, the flow of current returns to its normal path through the midline, and it allows the seeing process to open.

LONGING

The next possible bump in the road for some is one of longing; many people really want to see the auric field. However, in that "really wanting" is a discomfort, especially if you have not been allowed, haven't been given the opportunity, or you simply haven't had the knowledge to express the longing. So the longing gets stored in the body over time, often as a block form, a sticky area of energy in the field. If this situation applies, one option is to sink into this longing, allowing yourself to feel the "really wanting," if only for a split second; then the energy form will begin to change and move. It will be uncomfortable yet not painful physically or emotionally, and only temporarily so; but the act of contact is well worth the experience.

It is somewhat like a scary moment in a bad movie when your stomach tightens for a moment and then you realize it is not real. The sensation passes, the blocked energy clears, and you can move forward in your seeing.

Rage

The last of the common potential obstacles is rage. For many people "anger" at being able to see exists, because when one begins to be able to see, one begins to name Truth. In many families of origin, truth can be in short supply. When you see the field you often see the Truth, and not necessarily what people wish you to see. Over time, it becomes extremely difficult to lie. Saying nothing about what is seen is not hard. But lying about what you see becomes very difficult. So in making a commitment to see the auric field, one is fundamentally making a commitment to Truth, and Truth with a capital "T," not truth with a small "t." Not the truth of what you feel in day-to-day life may be true, but the real Truth -- the Truth of Life, and the Truth in the interactions between people.

What comes out of that Truth can be tremendous rage. It is rage that people aren't telling you the Truth, because you can see that what they're thinking in their field is different than what they're saying with their mouth. Rage that people would say, "No, I haven't been involved in this particular project or in this particular aspect," when in fact they have been involved in whatever situation about which you are concerned. You are responsible, when you begin seeing, for how you handle that rage. The best solution is to release the rage into the Earth as food/information for the earth. It is much like how a tree inhales carbon dioxide and exhales oxygen and we inhale the oxygen and exhale the carbon dioxide. It becomes a symbiotic process where the Earth gains information and you gain control. Let's move to the next section, which is the Ethics of Seeing, and discuss some of those aspects about the management of rage.

If you are feeling angry, you might consider
taking a walk in a beautiful setting.

CHAPTER ELEVEN

ETHICS OF SEEING

Seeing the auric field entails several responsibilities. First, there is the responsibility of confidentiality. As you begin to see the auric field, you will have access to a great deal of information which may be unknown to the person whose field you are looking at, and may be unknown to people around them. As someone involved in seeing the auric field, you have a responsibility, a requirement, to not share the information that you see about another person with anyone but that other person.

How you share the information which you perceive is also important. There are some basic guidelines for sharing information about the auric field. The first is, did the person ask you to tell them? If they didn't, generally, it's a good idea not to say anything. The second is if they have asked, and you are going to tell them, is the information that you are going to tell them the Truth? Is there any chance that you are making a mistake in your perception of this person's field, and the understanding of its delicate relationship to the whole of this person? **Verify the seeing with more than one sense.** Never say something as an absolute. It is your perception instead.

Remember, unless you are a physician or equivalent it is unethical for you to share information in/of a medical style because you are not qualified to make a medical diagnosis.

For example, if it looks as if there is a block around the heart chakra, which could potentially imply some sort of heart difficulty, can you see from the way that the person is physically moving that they are protecting the area? Do you hear a sound when you look at the field, not just see a cloud in front of the heart area? When you tune in to the person's behavior, do they appear very, very pressured? Can you tell if the person is a very "heart-centered" type of person? Take a careful analysis, a very careful look, before you go on to share the information. **Is it True?**

The next thing that you want to check: **Is it kind?** Is the way that you are going to express the information to another person a kind way? You want to be very sure, since you are providing information to this person, who may or may not have this condition, that you do it in such a way that you are gentle and supportive and thoughtful. It does not help either one of you if you provide the information in such a way that creates more anguish in the world.

The next thing that you want to consider is: **Does the person need to know the information?** Is this information that a person has to have? Many times when I look at someone's field, I receive a tremendous amount of information about that person. I share very, very, very little of that information with the person, unless specifically requested. If a person asks you, and you have verified that the information is correct, you must be willing to provide the information in a kind way; and if there is a need to know, then it's okay to share it.

Finally, you need to have a firm connection to **what do you gain by sharing the information?** Integrity of Self is a key mark, a hallmark to being able to see the auric field and being able to communicate what you see in others' auric fields. You are seeking after Truth. You are seeking after knowledge of "self," when you start to see and discover the auric field.

Since that is the case, use every time that you see another person's field as an opportunity to learn about yourself. And, in particular, when requested to communicate information about another person, use it as an opportunity to see how you work, and how your field works in reaction to the other person.

Similar to the way a bruise or trauma can look in the field of someone who is running.

The situation is similar to what you might see looking at the lines of light on a person's body when they are running. Do you see the spot marked with an arrow? That is similar to the way a bruise would look in the field. If you do not know them do you have the right to share this information? NO! What if you ask their "higher self"? NO! You may only share this directly with them and only if they give you verbal permission first.

As you ground and charge, clear and stimulate the third eye area, allow yourself to see. Watch what *your* field does as you provide the information about the other person's field to them. Does your field start to run a different way as you are speaking? Does the other person start to move into terror? Do you see streaks shooting out of their field? Do they appear physically agitated? What do you do in response? Do you stop speaking? Do you feel yourself withdraw? Do you relax? Do you become gentler? Do you become kinder? Notice what you are doing, because what you see in response to another person's field will teach you a great deal about you, and about your own auric field.

In addition to the ethics about speaking with someone, there are additional ethics around your responsibilities. First we've spoken about confidentiality, and we've spoken about the correct way to give information to another. You are also responsible for how you respond to the information that you see.

For example, if you see someone's energy field flowing toward another person's energy field, and one happens to be a man and the other a woman, it is both improper and unwise to share that information with those around you. Not only is it impolite to share that information generally, it may create a great deal of anger around you. So you want to be aware of what you're doing in response, what you personally take action on in response to what you see. **Can you share the information without judgment?**

One of the toughest lessons that many of my students experience as they begin to see, is being fearful of something triggering their own anger. What would they do then? The answer is, take action but *only when you're clear*. Take action in a way that is whole and kind and loving, *not* in a way that is vindictive, aggressive, or creates more trauma and stress. You have an obligation, when you're seeing the auric field, to respond in a manner that is kind, thoughtful, and supportive of those around you.

Another responsibility is to pick and choose your behavior with regard to the demand you may make on another person, to ask you for information, to want to hear it. Many of my students, in the process of developing their auric vision, will go through a period of time where they really want to show people that they have the skill which they have developed. They are actively seeking to create health and wellbeing for those around them by sharing the information which they see in the auric field. When you have the feeling that you would like to share the information about the auric field with someone else, stop and ask yourself, what is my motive here? What will I gain from doing this?

For example, if you are thinking, "Oh, I just want to show off," or "I really feel that they need the information because they appear to be ill in this particular area," when you are very clear on your motive and know that the information may be valuable to them, then you can make a wise choice. If you know that you are just showing off, caution yourself to wait for another opportunity. Don't worry, there will be an opportunity for you to share your information and your skills, but in a way that supports all of those around you and does not create a rhythm of just self-gain.

Another issue that often comes up for students as they are developing their vision is how to handle it when someone asks them for the information. They provide the information in good conscience, with integrity and as cleanly as they can; then the person responds negatively, saying that they are lying, or that what they have told them is not true. I suggest you answer with, "That may be how you feel, but I've told you what I'm seeing at this time."

Then terminate the conversation. Do not take the person's response personally. Allow for the fact that the information that you provided to them may be unsettling, or difficult for them to understand. In most cases where this happens, the person involved comes back in a week or two, sometimes longer, and acknowledges to you that you were right in some areas but perhaps off in others. Respond with "That's nice, thank you for the feedback; I appreciate it." Terminate the conversation and go on about your business. Allow the person to have the opportunity to have their personal experience of the information without making a judgment, one way or another, in response to their concern. Be as supportive as you can when you provide information to people, and be aware that many times the information that you provide will be a surprise, may create some concern or fear, but may also create some happiness, then or in the future.

The next obligation and responsibility is to express information in such a way that you balance the things that will create joy for the person, and the information that may create some concern. If you see a very dark cloud over the heart, and the person says, "I've been having some chest pain. Do you see anything in my field?" You might say, "Well, I do see some clouds in that general area. Have you seen a physician?" Or you might say, "Well, what you have done to explore the energy in that area? Have you been checked by a physician?" If the person says "no," you might say, "well, I see some clouding there; it might be wise to check it out." Again, I'm being kind and gentle. I'm not saying, "Your heart chakra is fully clouded, and you're going to have a heart attack." That would be extremely foolish, because I don't know that this is the Truth. Further, I am not a physician and I may not make a medical diagnosis. This person may change the clouding in the field the instant they become aware of it. Given the opportunity and the correct set of circumstances surrounding the time and place, anyone can change. Do be kind in how you express the information to the person. Say things gently, say things that are in Truth and in integrity of "self," and say things in a way that is compassionate.

As you develop seeing over time, you'll begin to see more and more information about each level of the auric field and dimensions, of the field other than the auric. As you start to move into the astral dimensions for example, the information that you see may be very surprising and very dramatic. You may get images. You may see pictures, with the astral or any other dimension, almost like those you would see on a television screen. Just watch and enjoy the experience and be responsible in your sharing!

QUICK RECAP ~ ETHICAL CHECK LIST

1. Is it true?
- If you are not sure then work from the position that it is not true and do not share the information until you are sure one way or the other.
2. Have you verified it with more than one sense?
- Be sure that you can verify the information with more than one sense.
3. Can another person verify your impressions?
- Get another opinion especially if you may not be clean in this area.
4. Is it kind?
- If you cannot say it in a way that is kind, do not tell the person.
5. Does the person need to know the information?
- If they do not need to know this information do not share it. If they do need to know the information share it with discernment.
6. What will you gain by sharing the information?
- Be very clear. You owe it to yourself not to create negative karma.
7. What will the client gain by receiving the information?
- Run possibilities in your head. Expect the unexpected.
8. Can you gift the information to the person in such a way that you say the words without blame and judgment?
- If you cannot do not say it until you can. Do your processing at home not in the session. The client is not your therapist.
9. Are you making a medical diagnosis? If so is it within your scope of practice?
10. Does the client have adequate support for the period that they are processing the information that you have provided to them?
- If they do not, see that they get some before you share.

CHAPTER TWELVE

OTHER METHODS OF PERCEIVING THE AURIC FIELD

As we mentioned in the last chapter, one of your responsibilities before providing information to someone is to check with other senses what you perceived the person's auric field. Did you perceive it with your physical eyes? Was there something in the way the person moved, or spoke? Was there something in the way the person was holding their arm or shoulder that would support what you saw in the auric field? Was there a sound associated with it, or a taste? What did it feel like as you felt out the other person? Check with more than one sense. There are a number of other methods of perceiving the auric field. They are:

- *Kinesthetic sense*
- *Hearing/sound*
- *Taste*
- *Smell*
- *Extended senses of touch*
- *Intuition*
- *A "knowing"*
- *And of course, sight!*

These are the normal five senses but with an interesting twist: each of these senses can perform the same type of functions as its counterparts. For example, you can listen with your nose, you can smell with your ear and taste with your eye, and you can see with your tongue. The most common practice is to use your senses individually in the beginning.

The first is called the kinesthetic sense. In the kinesthetic sense, one who is empathetic would feel what the other person is feeling. They would feel how the muscle feels. They would feel how the shoulder feels. They would feel how the heart feels. They actually perceive what is happening in the other person's body and physically feel the same problem within themselves. Over time, they perceive it physically inside the other person.

The next way is to hear the auric field. Not only can you hear with your ears, but also with your expanded and extended senses. For example, it's possible to watch a sunset and hear a sunset at the same time. They always sound like a Beethoven symphony to me. If you are using your ears to hear on the auric layers it is possible to look at a block and hear a sound that the block is making. It is possible to look at a piece of food and hear the symphony of a baked potato. Each and every thing that you will come into contact with, each and every being that you will come in contact with, each and every person that you will come in contact with has a multitude of sounds associated with them.

Over time you develop an internal set of frequencies that you know mean particular things in your terms of perception. For example, when I hear a block on the G two octaves above middle C, then I know that is the sound of the person screaming in the auric field. Another example: when I am listening in the field, and I begin to hear a dialogue associated with a block, I know that there is a conversation that actually took place at the time that block got stored. In that situation I get an opportunity to hear the sequence of events, the dialogues that took place. Sometimes it will only be a sentence or a phrase, but oftentimes that will be a key phrase. Here is an example: in viewing a field of a person, I found a wonderful rose-colored cloud. This was a person who was challenging the issue of over eating. In the center of that cloud was the work "eat" in black. When I listened to the sound that the "eat" made, I heard the voice of the person's mother. It was a very interesting experience. You are able to gain a great deal of information by listening to the field.

So let us suppose there is a block in someone's field. This block happens to be yellow-green. In my personal seeing language the color tells me that this is a jealousy-related block. When I taste it ethereally, it tastes bitter with an overtone of sour. It is a cross between a lemon and a lime. It's a very specific taste that over the years I have learned to associate actively with a block or with a sound that's associated with jealousy. In this way I have verified my visual perception with one associated with taste.

In addition to the kinesthetic sense, the sense of hearing and the sense of taste, there is also the sense of smell. When I see a block, I take a sniff. What does it smell like? You can have a great pink cloud, which is the color of love, and inside it have a deep black center that you won't see until you peel away the pink cloud. The pink cloud is to protect the person from the black vibration. But, if I touch into the pink cloud, and take a sniff, I will very often smell a kind of putrid and fetid overtone. I have known that when I get that overtone there is an internal component, the black part hidden in the pink of the cloud, which is providing protection to the person. The block is something that the person needs to become aware of over time. In helping this person become aware of this block I mention something that's in relationship to it, just in normal dialogue, or I might discuss a situation that may have been similar in my life. This discussion might allow the awareness of the person's own experience to come to mind. In turn this gives them an opportunity to reexamine it.

Another way that you can use the sense of smell is to take a sniff of a whole field layer. A smell of jasmine is a lovely smell that you can find in the field. You find it particularly when you are on the higher layers (fifth and above) of the auric field. It's a wonderful and comforting smell for me. It feels as if I'm coming home.

Often when you have a connection to a person's field and you begin to see a block, that block starts rolling back in time. You observe a system and then the system begins to change. If you smell, taste, and listen, as well as watch the block roll back in time, like a movie, you'll have an opportunity to gain some beautiful perceptions using those senses. Ask yourself: what did this moment taste like to this person? What did this moment sound like to this person? What did this moment smell like to the person? It can be a delicious smell and a delightful experience.

In addition to developing the kinesthetic sense, the feeling out of the other person, the smell, taste, hearing, and vision, you can also have an extended sense of touch. Some people mix a kinesthetic feeling touch and a kinesthetic touch sense. But the two are different. Each contains overtones of the other, but in fact they feel to me as if they are different senses. One is an empathetic response, and the other is a visceral response. So you can have extended senses of touch.

A fun example of this might be when you're trying to find your car keys. You can run you fingers under the cushions to see if there is anything hard and cold, or sharp under there. You could run your auric fingertips, not your physical fingertips, under the cushions. You can walk your auric fingertips across the carpet with your eyes closed, and find something that's lying on the carpet. Better yet, check behind that hard-to-reach cabinet, and see whether or not a bracelet, a piece of paper, a business card, or something else has fallen behind it. Then you know whether or not you need to move it to find the object. You do that simply by tuning into your auric field layers, and using them to reach out and run your hands behind the particular piece of furniture.

You can practice it in this way. First ground and charge. Then allow yourself to really feel one of your two hands. Allow yourself to focus your mind, and then using imagination as a tool, imagine your fingers walking across the tabletop in the other room. What's on the table? Let's explore it. Do you find anything wet? Is the surface dry? Is there anything that's warm or cold? Your fingertips will feel it. Feel as if you're reaching out your hand, spilling the energy from your heart layer into your hand, reaching it out, and walking those fingertips right across the table. It's a lovely process, and lots of fun. It's a great game to play with children, and they're very, very good at it. The younger the better, and at two or three they are absolute pros! They can feel everything that's on that table in the other room, better than they will be able to tell you what's on the table in that same room.

In addition to the primary extended senses, there are senses that some people call "sixth" senses, that of intuition, and that of knowing. Intuition and knowing are two very different things, and they are different from your thinking mind. Remember, the purpose of the mind is to notice a pattern, recognize a pattern happening again, and allow the energies to be focused, to use the mind as a recorder and focus point. The heart should make the choices of life. The mind just recognizes a choice point. So when I talk about intuition, I'm talking again of a sense similar to the kinesthetic sense.

It's an awareness. You may perhaps experience it as a discomfort, or a sense of knowing that something's coming. It's an awareness that something is about to change or it just doesn't feel right. Most people sense this if they walk into a room where a very intense meeting has just taken place. You can walk in and even though everyone may be quiet, you know that it wasn't necessarily happy, because your stomach starts to do flip-flops. That is this sense of knowing that something just isn't right, but you don't know why, and no one has told you.

Think about a particular topic, the birth of the Universe. The knowing about the birth of the Universe would encompass the whole process of perception, the whole concept in a single moment. One of my friends is particularly good at this. This person has the ability to, if you explain the topic, open up the channel, and receive information in the fullest sense of the word. When the person is done receiving the information, it's as if they know all about it, and are suddenly a historian. It's a very wonderful sense, and one to be treasured.

In addition to your ordinary senses that are extended, you can also do some very interesting things just using the heart layer, the fourth layer of the auric field. As I mentioned before, the fourth layer of the field is a very fluid and beautifully colored layer. The heart has its own sense of hearing, taste, touch, smell, and vision. In my experience, you can see with your heart. You can hear with your heart. You can smell with your heart. Any mother who has taken a child out of a mud puddle who is thoroughly dirty, from one end to the other, and very, very smelly, has turned on smelling with the heart in order to get through the next ten minutes, until the child is scrubbed. Again, these are extended senses, but specific to the fourth layer of the field.

The fourth level is the level of love. When one hears with the heart, one hears love even inside words that are filled with pain and anger. There is a loving heart behind them, and one that truly seeks to make a connection to the other or the emotional response would not be so strong. If one sees with the heart, one sees that no matter how a person is configured, tall or short, wide or slim, twisted or straight, that the person is beautiful. The star that shines within them, the soul that is bright and a beacon within them, is always beautiful.

When one tastes with the heart, it tastes gentle and delicate. There are overtones of the sweetness of the Universe, and it is truly joyous. Imagine that your heart is opening up, and feels like a flower. And imagine that flower has a honeybee walking on it. What is the taste of the honeybee from the flower's point of view? It's a fun thing to try. Allow yourself to imagine this and then let yourself taste. Let yourself taste with your heart, and see what happens.

One of the fun things that you can do, too, is touch people with the heart. The fields come into contact with each other and begin pulse in synchronicity. If you will allow yourself to make contact with the other person's heart, you can touch your heart to theirs. It almost looks as if a little tendril, not a cord, but a tendril of light comes from the heart, and touches the heart of the other. It pours pure light of love into the other but it doesn't stay, it withdraws. However, it allows for moments of contact that are truly from the heart and is a deeply joyous process.

Let yourself discover this wonderful universe of sensing that is available to people in human form. Enjoy!

QUICK RECAP!

1. Begin to breathe a very deep breath, and release it.
2. Next, you need to be grounded. This is like plugging yourself into an electrical socket to acquire the necessary power to clear the "midline current."
3. Set any intentions to perceive which you wish.
4. Then start to charge and clear the midline current. It is in the center of the body, and flows from the bottom of the torso through the top of the head, straight up the midline of the body.
5. Since many people do not have a clear flow of current straight up the body, I encourage them to add two specific arcs of current to the process. Start with an arc of gold current from the first chakra going up the front of the body and into the front of the sixth chakra. Once that flow is solid, add an arc of rose current from the tip of the coccyx (tailbone) to the back of the sixth chakra.
6. Next, you charge the sixth and seventh chakras, so that there is a large amount of energetic flow in through the area.
7. Clear any blocks that may be in the way of that flow of the current.
8. Switch up from looking through your physical eyes to looking through the eye of the forehead.
9. See what you can see!

Final Review

Let's review quickly, one more time, the exact process that you must go through to see the auric field:

First, *breathe*. The breath is the fire, the breath is the flow, and breath is the current that generates the power, which allows you to see. Then *ground*. Allow energy from the earth to flow into your body and help power your seeing. Set an intention if you choose to do so. Allow the midline power current to clear. Allow the sixth and seventh chakras to clear. Spin the sixth and seventh chakras.

Arc light in front of the first chakra in through the front of the sixth. Arc rose light from the back of the first chakra at the coccyx, into the back of the sixth chakra. Let the current run quickly, and in fact if you can, let the current double. Next, switch to looking through your forehead, with your eyes open or closed to begin with, then open your eyes and see what you see.

Enjoy the process!

If you have any fear, any anger, any feeling that you need to control the other person, come up, stop, work on the reasons that you are having that issue appear and then start at the beginning again with the breath. Always *remember the ethics*; know that you are responsible for your actions. The moment you make the case to speak to someone, the effect is inherent in that cause. You will get a response. You may not get it at the same moment, but you will get a response.

As we close on this material, I would like to remind you of a couple of specific things, in addition to the process. Just as when the pebble is dropped into the stream, the ripples reach out across the pond. The ripple bounces the lily pad, surprises the frog and the frog jumps into the water. The splash of the water startles the bird that is feeding on the bugs in the shallows. The bird flies into the sky. The whole process of the peaceful pond is shifted. We are shifted as we begin to see. The world is a different place because our perceptions are different.

Remember, *fear is the biggest hindrance* to seeing the field. Clearing the fear makes the whole process easier, and there will be many times that you will return to that place of needing to clear that fear as you drop to a deeper level of understanding, and a cleaner and clearer ability to perceive the field. Remember, *compassion toward self and patience toward self*, so that you do this process in smaller steps. It is less common for someone to perceive the field fully in a single session. It is more common for someone to move gently, softly into a place of perceiving the field in stages. Remember to *have fun with the process*. It really can be joyous and wondrous as one perceives and deepens the receiving or seeing process.

I leave you with the thought with which we began: *the element of breath*. I cannot stress it strongly enough. The breath is the fire. The breath is the flow. The breath creates the current, which powers the process of seeing the auric field.

I would like to leave you with a hope.
May all of your seeing create value and beauty.

Cactus at Dawn

I hope that you will journey gently and with wisdom and use these skills with honor and integrity.

ABOUT THE AUTHOR

Melinda H. Connor

Beginning her training as a child in the energy skills, she is the founder of Earthsongs Holistic Consulting & Executive Director of the International Journal of Healing & Caring. She is the lineage holder for the Resonance Modulation energy skills training program. Between Harvard, Wellesley, University of San Francisco, California Coast University, University of Arizona, American Military University and seminary programs, she holds three master's degrees and two doctorates.

Dr. Connor was trained in research as an NIH T-32 postdoctoral fellow in the Program in Integrative Medicine from the University of Arizona. Professor Connor, is the former chair of the board of directors for the National Alliance of Energy Practitioners and is also both nationally certified by NCCOEP and board certified by the American Alternative Medicine Association.

She is a lifetime fellow of the Royal Society of Medicine in the UK, professor emerita and former research director at Akamai University, and the author of ten books. Professor Connor has received both international awards from *CEO Today Magazine* and *Finance Monthly* and US recognition from the *California State Legislative Assembly*. Named a top research scientist by the World Qigong Congress and Marquis Who's Who, she was recently bestowed with the prestigious title of Empowered Woman of the Year for 2024 by the International Association of Top Professionals (IAOTP). This recognition is a testament to her outstanding leadership, unwavering dedication, and unparalleled commitment to the industry.

WWW.DRMELINDAHCONNOR.COM
WWW.EARTHSONGS.COM
WWW.IJHC.ORG

www.ingramcontent.com/pod-product-compliance
Lightning Source LLC
Chambersburg PA
CBHW072152160426
43197CB00012B/2358